Seymond D.

Seymond D. Perry, Sr
Do You
Love Me
God's Question to Mankind

Do You Love Me?

God's Question to Mankind

Unless otherwise stated, Scripture references are taken from the King James Version of the Holy Bible.

ISBN 13: 978-1945117022
ISBN 10: 1945117028
Library of Congress Control Number: 2016935430

For information and bulk ordering, contact:
Pearly Gates Publishing LLC
Angela R. Edwards, CEO
P.O. Box 62287
Houston, TX 77205
BestSeller@PearlyGatesPublishing.com

DEDICATIONS

This book is dedicated to my loving wife, Sarah Perry, and my dear children, Dontre' and Sean. In the midst of darkness and despair, they loved me - even when I did not love myself. From the ashes, they helped me to see and embrace the love of Jesus again.

This book is also dedicated to my mother, Clara Perry, and my deceased father, George Perry. As my devoted parents, they were the first to show and exemplify God's powerful and limitless love.

ACKNOWLEDGEMENTS

Above all else, I want to acknowledge my Lord and Savior Jesus Christ. Without Him, I would have no life; without Him, I would be utterly helpless and useless; without Him, this body of work would not be possible.

Secondly, I would like to acknowledge my pastor, Alvin Robertson, and my *Kingdom of God Ministries* family. It is because of this ministry that my life has been rescued from the brink of destruction. It is because of how this godly group of believers allowed the Holy Spirit to flow through them that I am able to stand as the man of God I am today.

Last, but not least, I want to acknowledge my loving wife. She is such a joy and sorrow, pleasure and annoyance, peace and chaos. She pushes me, drives me, and gives me what I need to become all God has called me to be. For the countless nights I've stayed awake…for the emotional distance…for my inability to verbalize my thoughts…and for putting up with my high energy level…THANKS! You may not be the wife I asked for, but you are exactly who I **needed**. Sarah, I love you with the love of Jesus.

PREFACE

The journey of writing this book was not very easy. In fact, it was somewhat difficult and spiritually taxing. Due to my disobedience, I lost a great deal chasing the cares of this world while unsuccessfully trying to fulfill my immoral lusts and foolish pride. I've lost time, money, and even portions of my career have suffered. Most importantly, during those times, I've lost fellowship with God; for it is sin that always separates us from the Lord.

Shame overwhelms me when I think that I chose sin and pleasure over my relationship with God. The failure of a leader usually results in consequences far more grave than the fall of a non-leader. For example, Scripture tells us that on the day Aaron (a leader) failed, *"...about 3,000 men died..."* (Exodus 32:27-28). When leaders fall, followers also pay the price. Therefore, I was not the only one who suffered through my ordeals. My family and those closest to me paid a great price for my mistakes.

It is almost unspeakable, but my wife and children have borne the weight the most behind my stupidity. Still today, my family is suffering the consequences behind my shortcomings. Many times, in the still of the night, I've cried bitter tears of sorrow. *"Only if..." "What if...?" "Why can't I...?"* and countless other rants would resound through my mind with a deafening echo - so loud at times, I thought myself to be insane. The thought of my sin was so great, I knew **only** the Lord could deliver and restore me.

None of those things had to be. They were caused (admittedly) by my foolish actions. **My** arrogance, **my** pride, **my** lust, and **my** disobedience has brought such a calamity to my life. My home, job, church, and even my heart have been in utter chaos because of my decisions. The Lord is truly gracious towards us; *however*, after being warned by the Lord time and time again, His mercy finally ended and judgment began. I was dealt a **mighty** blow from the hand of God.

At times, I felt as if someone was sitting on my chest, forcing the very life from every pore of my body.

At times, I felt like a lonely, fatherless child…alone, ashamed, and defenseless.

At times, I felt like a man wandering through the desert…starving, thirsty, overworked, and in desperate need of a savior.

Even in those dark and gloomy moments, God's Word would continue to be a lamp unto my feet and a light unto my path. My heart would soon ring with the words of the psalmist, *"I would've fainted unless I hoped to see the kindness of the Lord in the land of the living"* (Psalm 27:13).

I soon discovered that even at my lowest moment, the Lord remained faithful and true to me. It shall never cease to amaze me how the One who is the same yesterday, today, and forever always keeps His promises. Though seasons change, though cultures change, and though we (as people) change, the God of Heaven and Earth never changes. The very words He spoke to me to secure my eternal salvation are the same words the Lord spoke to me at that junction in my life. God promised that even in my lowest, most sinful, evil, darkest, and desperately wicked state, *"I will never leave you nor forsake you."* Oh, what **JOY** those words brought to my soul!

If only for a brief moment, there seemed to be light at the end of the tunnel. In the midst of my dark gloom and despair, the loving arms of God held me close, comforted me, and revealed to me the words that are to follow:

Love is attachment, intimate fellowship, and loyal devotion. It is a selfless, sacrificial service to others that seeks the best for them. It is love that God demands in His law: "Love the Lord your God...and love your neighbor as yourself" (Matthew 22:37-39). The Lord Himself is Love, for everything He does is characterized by love.

In that moment – in the presence of God and His angels – Jesus asked me, ***"Do you love Me or do you love this world?"***

Uncontrollable streams of water began to flow from my eyes. Like never before, I then realized that my love for God was lacking...and my love for the world was far too great.

"Love not the world, neither the things that are in the world. If any man love the world, the love of the Father is not in him. For all that is in the world, the lust of the flesh, and the lust of the eyes, and the pride of life, is not of the Father, but is of the world.
And the world passeth away, and the lust thereof: but he that doeth the will of God abideth forever."
(1 John 2:15-16)

INTRODUCTION

Part of the arrogance of human nature is to think that we know more than others do. That truth is evident in the lives of countless people every day. In the First Epistle of John, the apostle addresses the problem of false teachers who were making lofty claims about their knowledge regarding the deity and nature of Christ. John counters their false claims by reminding his readers of the eyewitness accounts of the apostles, including himself. Jesus Christ came in human flesh, lived a human life, died, and then was raised from the dead. He was fully human…and fully GOD! Anything else being taught by others was false. In his letter, John sounded the alarm: False teaching could not be tolerated! Falsehoods would lead to immorality, and immorality would lead to eternal death. In contrast, the truth would demonstrate itself in love, and love would lead to eternal life. That is why it is paramount that we love God and not the world - for our lives, movement, and very beings are directly tied to our love for the Father.

Christians must not allow themselves to become affected by the attitudes and behaviors of the unbelievers around them. The unbelieving people of the world (the unbeliever's frame of mind primarily relates to the world system) belong to the age of darkness and make their decisions according to what they want for themselves - whether concerning possessions, activities, achievements, or status.

Believers often act in a way that is inconsistent with their relationship with Christ. The world around us - radio, television, magazines, Internet, and newspapers - all influence us to believe and behave like the world. As such, *"Love not the world"* may be rephrased to read ***"Stop loving the world"***. Why? Because the world (which is full of evil desires, lusts or pleasures, and pride) is utterly hated by our Heavenly Father. That is why God instructs us to stay away from those things. Someday, all that He hates (sin) will be destroyed. The Word declares that the world and everything attached to it will someday pass away (1 John 2:17). Therefore, if we are attached to the world, then we shall pass away as well. The Father and the world cannot be loved together. As Jesus profoundly taught, *"You will love the one, and hate the other, but you will not love both"* (Matthew 6:24).

The present world is passing away even now. Living in this temporary world, one must not love it (2 Timothy 4:10), become conformed to its ways (Romans 12:2), or fall in love with its godless "wisdom" (James 3:15). Every day, however, we see many who make those fatal mistakes: those who choose money over the Savior…those who choose family and friends over the Word…and those who choose the world over sweet fellowship with God's Holy Spirit. In fact, we can be included in that number. Any time we choose what we want as opposed to God's wants, we have chosen our own selfish lusts.

Instead, we must choose to live a godly life. We must avoid the snares of the "present evil age" from which Christ's death has set His people free. "The world" is hostile towards God. "The world" is full of corruption and stands as a symbol of perversion.

Though I have made this statement previously, it cannot be overemphasized: You cannot be friends with this evil world and love God at the same time (James 4:4). By their faith, believers must "overcome the world" by killing whatever belongs to their "earthly nature" and denying "worldly passions" (Titus 2:12).

TABLE OF CONTENTS

IS SOMETHING MISSING IN YOUR LIFE?

My friend, are you dead or alive? Do you ever feel that there is something important missing from your life? Is there a vital part of your existence that isn't there - and has never been there? Is there an empty void and a longing deep within the depths of your soul, crying out to be filled?

If you do not know the Lord, Jesus Christ, on a personal basis, that is the problem. God - the Giver and Sustainer of life - is missing from your life. The Bible says without Jesus Christ as your personal Savior, you are *"dead in trespasses and sins"* (Ephesians 2:5).

How Did It Happen?

In the beginning, before man's fall, Adam and Eve were alive - that is, they were "spiritually" alive. They walked in perfection and oneness with God. Adam and Eve enjoyed a flawless relationship with the Lord.

"And the LORD God commanded the man, saying, "Of every tree of the garden, thou mayest freely eat: But of the tree of the knowledge of good and evil, thou shalt not eat of it: for in the day that thou eatest thereof, thou shalt surely die" (Genesis 2:16-17).

When they disobeyed God and ate of the fruit, they died a "physical" and "spiritual" death. Sin entered in, and they were separated from God. Since then, everyone has inherited or been born into sin. The results of sin are a spiritual death, a physical death, and (if you die without Christ) an eternal death. The eternal death is separation from God in Hell…for all of eternity.

"For the wages of sin is death; but the gift of God is eternal life through Jesus Christ our Lord" (Romans 6:23).

What's Been Done About It?

Jesus Christ (God in the form of man) was not a partaker of man's sinful bloodline. He was perfect, sinless, righteous, holy, born of a virgin, and God in flesh.

"That which was from the beginning, which we have heard, which we have seen with our eyes, which we have looked upon, and our hands have handled, of the Word of life; (For the life was manifested, and we have seen it, and bear witness, and shew unto you that eternal life, which was with the Father, and was manifested unto us); That which we have seen and heard declare we unto you, that ye also may have fellowship with us: and truly our fellowship is with the Father, and with His Son Jesus Christ" (1 John 1-3).

"And the Word was made flesh, and dwelt among us, (and we beheld His glory, the glory as of the only begotten of the Father), full of grace and truth" (John 1:14).

Jesus came to seek and to save the lost. He offered Himself as the perfect, sinless sacrifice unto God, to redeem man from the sin which separates us from God. He came to give life back to mankind.

"Verily, verily, I say unto you, He that heareth my Word, and believeth on Him that sent me, hath everlasting life, and shall not come into condemnation; but is passed from death unto life. Verily, verily, I say unto you, The hour is coming, and now is, when the dead shall hear the voice of the Son of God: and they that hear shall live" (John 5:24-25).

Now, It Is Up to You!

In Romans 5:8, God says *"Christ died for us"*. Jesus paid the price for our sins. He died and shed His blood in our place. God says if we will admit that we are sinners, believe that Jesus paid for our sins with His own blood, and receive Him by faith, He will give us eternal life.

"That if thou shalt confess with thy mouth the Lord Jesus, and shalt believe in thine heart that God hath raised Him from the dead, thou shalt be saved. For with the heart man believeth unto righteousness; and with the mouth confession is made unto salvation" (Romans 10:9-10).

Will you agree with God that you need to be saved and receive Jesus Christ as your personal Savior right now?

My 1st Love Letter to God

(Use this section to be honest with both God and yourself. Tell God why you LOVE HIM, what you need forgiveness for, and why you are grateful.)

THE LUST OF THE FLESH

"For all that is in the world, the lusts of the flesh…is not of the Father, but is of the world."

1 John 2:16

"The toughest part of turning around a bad situation is realizing and admitting that you were wrong."

~ The 4th Secret of the One Minute Manager

How do I begin to explain the lust of the flesh? In Christianity, the word "flesh" is used as a metaphor to describe our fallen nature or sinful tendencies. It denotes mere human nature, the earthly nature of man apart from divine influence, and therefore prone to sin and opposed to God. Very simply, your flesh is everything about you minus God. The Bible clearly tells us in numerous ways that our flesh is enemy with God. If we follow our flesh (our natural will and desires), we will ultimately be following the path of death (Galatians 6:8).

In a church I once attended, an old deacon often reminded us that everyone must be taught how to live righteous and godly lives; but no one must be taught how to do what's wrong. We are born with that innate instinct. It's not easy to tell our bodies "no" when every fiber of our being cries "YES!" Our flesh is what we know; it is what we are most comfortable with. From the moment we exit our mother's womb, there is a certain desperation to satisfy our flesh. Even as we move through the various phases of life, that hunger is only fed to become more and more insatiable.

It is not until salvation that we become aware of the spirit realm. It is not until the Holy Spirit enters our hearts that we truly become illuminated to the truth of the eternal…not just the temporal.

As long as I can remember, I've battled with certain physical cravings on one level or another. It started very early in life. Amazingly, I've carried some of those diseases into my regenerated life. I cringe to think of the lengths I've gone in order to please my flesh. I'm ashamed and utterly embarrassed when I recall the times I've denied Christ for self-gratification. If only I could go to those same great lengths to please my Heavenly Father. If only I could move self aside and live a life controlled by the Holy Spirit, then maybe...just maybe...I could overcome my sin issues.

Every day, my soul says, "Yes, Lord!", while my flesh cries, "No, Lord; not now." Nevertheless, we cannot fall into a self-induced depression. The enemy would love nothing better. We must realize mistakes are a part of life. Successful Christians recognize their errors, learn from them, and then work to correct their faults. Though we are to deal with those habits of ungodliness, we must not try to do it in our own strength (Ephesians 6:10).

Breaking sinful habits must be done in cooperation with the Holy Spirit and in dependence upon Him. Therefore, in dependence on the Holy Spirit, we must systematically work at acquiring the habit of saying "no" to the sins that so easily entangle us. The more we succeed in saying "no" to our sinful desires, the easier it becomes to say "no"!

With that being said, it is not wrong to have physical desires (hunger, sleep, relief from pain...and even sex), for they were all designed by God. It is sinful when we engage in those activities outside of the will of God. Too much food, too much sleep, drugs, and premarital sex are all outside of the Lord's will. Hence, they all fall into the category of the "lust of the flesh".

A Lost Inheritance

The main story of Genesis is God's plan to bless all nations through Abraham's descendants (Genesis 12). The great joy in that blessing is that it includes you and me! It begins with God's call to Abram and Sarai (Abraham and Sarah) to become the parents of a new people - a new nation. (Take note: Whenever God wants to do a work, He always begins with the leader.) The nation would become God's tool for blessing all peoples. As it related to Abram and Sarai, "the people" became the nation of Israel. Even though Abram and Sarai were merely an elderly couple with the means to travel, God chose to begin His plan of redemption for the entire world through them.

This should give great hope to any and all who may be facing unproductive, ancient, impossible, and even dead situations. You are never too far gone to be used by the Master; your limitations are never too great to be used by Him. With this in mind, the awesome Creator of the entire universe freely chose to make everlasting promises to Abraham and his descendants. Genesis is not merely a beginning. It provides the foundation for the rest of the biblical narrative.

"And Jacob sod pottage: and Esau came from the field, and he was faint: And Esau said to Jacob, "Feed me, I pray thee, with that same red pottage; for I am faint": therefore, was his name called Edom. And Jacob said, "Sell me this day thy birthright." And Esau said, "Behold, I am at the point to die; and what profit shall this birthright do to me?" And Jacob said, "Swear to me this day"; and he sware unto him: and he sold his birthright unto Jacob. Then Jacob gave Esau bread and pottage of lentiles; and he did eat and drink, and rose up, and went his way: thus Esau despised his birthright" (Genesis 25:29-34).

Esau, as the firstborn, had a birthright to a double portion of the family estate. Moreover, he inherited from his father (Isaac) the privilege of an everlasting covenant with God (Genesis 12:1-3); but Esau lost his birthright, which included God's gracious promises, by despising it and valuing the pleasure of food over it (Hebrews 12:16). Because Esau hungered so greatly, he was willing to give up anything to satisfy his stomach (a mere physical need). It is most unfortunate that he gave up his most valuable possession; his inheritance (both physical and spiritual blessings). We, too, give away our spiritual inheritance whenever we choose our flesh over obedience to the Lord.

One of my favorite scriptures about money is found in Malachi 3:10-11. It gives us one of the many birthrights of the believer. God promises to bless us abundantly if we would bring our tithes and offerings to Him. The Lord God Almighty tells us to "try Him in this matter". The word can mean "to test" in the sense of separating or discriminating one thing from another (Job 34:3). Malachi's challenge to the Israelites to try God is a rare instance in which people are encouraged to test the faithfulness of the Lord. How many of us are receiving that abundance? How many of us have no more room to receive? If most of us would be honest, we still suffer lack and do hunger. By being disobedient to God's commandments, could it be that we have given our inheritance to Satan? Could it be that God desires to bless, but we keep giving it away? The next time the enemy tempts you to sell your inheritance, hold on to your most valuable possession; your spiritual birthright.

Given to you upon your spiritual rebirth are all spiritual blessings in heavenly places. It is a priceless treasure. It is the one thing you can count on because it is backed by God's Word.

The Fall of Solomon

The Book of 1st Kings records the lives of a number of famous people - both good and evil. King David, King Solomon, and the Queen of Sheba are famous examples of righteous people searching after God's wisdom. They are people we can truly model our lives after.

On the other hand, Ahab and Jezebel are two notorious examples of wicked people discarding God's law and rebelling against Him. They are the type of people we consistently see around us (and sometimes, we behave like them). To confront a man as wicked as Ahab, God sent someone more than equal to the difficult task: the prophet Elijah. Often described as Israel's greatest and most dramatic prophet, Elijah displayed in an unforgettable way the amazing power of God over the false god Baal and his 400 prophets at Mount Carmel.

In the final analysis, 1st Kings is the story of one people headed down two very different paths. It is a story of good kings and bad kings, true prophets and false prophets, and of loyalty and disobedience to God. Most importantly, it is a story of Israel's spiritual odyssey and God's faithfulness to His people.

"But King Solomon loved many strange women, together with the daughter of Pharaoh, women of the Moabites, Ammonites, Edomites, Zidonians, and Hittites: Of the nations concerning which the LORD said unto the children of Israel, "Ye shall not go in to them, neither shall they come in unto you: for surely they will turn away your heart after their gods: Solomon clave unto these in love. And he had seven hundred wives, princesses, and three hundred concubines: and his wives turned away his heart. For it came to pass, when Solomon was old, that his wives turned away his heart after other gods: and his heart was not perfect with the LORD his God, as was the heart of David his father. For Solomon went after Ashtoreth the goddess of the Zidonians, and after Milcom the abomination of the Ammonites. And Solomon did evil in the sight of the LORD, and went not fully after the LORD, as did David his father" (1 Kings 11:1-6).

Near the beginning of Solomon's reign, Solomon asked for wisdom - and God answered abundantly (1 Kings 3:9-14). The Bible tells us that Solomon's wisdom exceeded that of all other men. By the end of his reign, this brilliant king somehow forgot the first principle of wisdom: *"The fear of the Lord is the beginning of wisdom…"* (Psalm 111:10). Somehow, somewhere along the way, Solomon lost sight of that golden spiritual truth.

Although some of Solomon's marriages were for political purposes, most of his wives and concubines were probably given as gifts. In the Hebrew text, the author emphasizes the word 'foreign', with a secondary emphasis on the adjective 'many'. Solomon had committed to egregious sins. Taking foreign wives violated the Lord's prohibitions against marrying Canaanite women (Deuteronomy 7:1-3). Those women usually brought their gods into Israel, and Solomon's weakness in worshipping those gods finally led to his horrendous downfall. God was not pleased with either act, but the first mistake was that the women did not serve the true and living God.

Any time we link our lives with individuals who and possessions that are not God-centered, we catapult our lives into the hands of the enemy. So, ask yourself: What have I joined myself to that is luring me away from God? Secondly, taking many wives violated the standard of monogamy established at the beginning. Each husband should have one wife; each wife should have one husband. So should it be with our souls. Each Christian should have one God, and God should have one cohesive unit of believers. Usually, however, that is not the case. We attempt to serve God and all the other gods of this world. We believe we can live "our lives" through the week and live for God when it's convenient. That does not trick or impress the Almighty in the least.

Jesus clearly instructs us: We cannot have two masters. Therefore, in particular areas of our lives, the Father is either Lord of all - or not at all. We may allow Him to be Lord at home, but not over our finances. He may be Lord over our jobs, but not over our health and physical fitness. We may allow Him to be Lord in our ministries, but not over our sexual addictions and frustrations. We must allow Jesus Christ to be Lord of every area of our lives: He must be Lord of all! We must surrender all to Him. Yes, that is easier said than done...but it is well worth it to see Jesus glorified in our lives.

The type of love Solomon possessed for his wives stems from the Hebrew word 'ahab', which refers to romantic love and covenant loyalty. That type of love speaks of being stuck to the other person or object. You can think of it as being joined together.

One of many of Solomon's problems was that he followed hard after the women in a covenant relationship. Because they were women not following after God (and Solomon was now "tied" to them), his heart was doomed to be led astray. There was nothing wrong with the people themselves, but the Lord didn't want His children to associate with them because He knew their hearts.

Throughout the Bible, God says to not associate with a particular people - and it's not because of race, color, creed, or nationality. He tells us not to associate with them because they do not have a relationship with Him. He tells us not to associate with them because they do not have a heart for the things of God.

Retrospectively, the Lord has instructed me countless times to stay away from "a thing"... and continually, I have chosen "it" over God. Like Solomon, it always ends in sheer chaos and destruction. Many times, I was left wondering: Why do I continue to choose death over life? Why would I continue to choose poison over health? Until now, I did not understand that this is what my flesh desires. Until I fully give those areas over to our Fortress (Psalm 18:2), I will repeatedly fall flat on my face. Until I allow Him to be Lord over every area, I will continue to have heartache and disappointment.

Even King David did not always live up to God's standard - that is truth; but he was loyal to God and trusted him implicitly, even when he was rebuked for his sins. Because of the influence of his many wives, Solomon compromised his faith by worshipping foreign gods. Today, the warning for God's people remains the same. In the Old Testament, God instructed the nation of Israel to keep the lamps in the temple lit throughout the day and night. Only the very best olive oil was to be burned in the lamps. However, the people became complacent in their devotion to the Lord and began burning cheaper oil. As a result, smoke filled the temple, blackening its walls.

That is what happens to us when we fail to keep ourselves pure before the Lord. We think our association with the world will not harm us, but it blackens our lives - then the clarity and brightness of God's life within us are dimmed. For this reason, we cannot live to our full spiritual potential in Him. Ask Him to reveal to you any impurity in your life so He can remove it and help you begin living clean in a dirty world.

Scripture tells us our God is a jealous God. He even instructs us that we should have no other god before Him. When the Bible says that we should fully follow the Lord, that's exactly what it means. Far too often, we are "double-minded" in our service to the Lord. A double-minded man should never expect to receive anything from the Lord, for that man is not in faith. It is only through faith that we please the Lord. It is only through faith that we serve Him. It is only through faith that we can truly and wholeheartedly love the Lord.

We often follow and serve sports, personal ambitions, family, and even career goals. With all your heart, with your entire mind, with all your body, and with your complete soul, you must serve God! Wholly, completely, and with abundance, we must commit to serving the Lord. Does that mean we will not make mistakes? No! All of us make mistakes - redeemed and unredeemed. It does mean, however, that when we do make mistakes, we won't cover them up, make excuses, or be unwilling to repent. Repentance derives from a Greek compound of 'meta' (after) and suggesting some type of change, and 'nous' (mind). The word strictly denotes "a change of mind". It also connotes remorse for sin - accompanied by a desire to turn away from one's sin, towards God, for salvation. At the moment of conviction, a consecrated heart will run back to Father God asking, *"What must I do to be saved?"* A heart that is quick to repent is a true sign of a maturing believer.

In the Beginning - Good for Food

"And when the woman saw that the tree was good for food..." Genesis 3:6

Eve, being near the tree while looking at it wishfully (as Satan attacked), could not discern anything in the fruit of the tree which showed it to be bad and unfit to be eaten. Neither could she comprehend why it should be forbidden for food. On the contrary, it had a most promising aspect: to be very delicious, nourishing, and beneficial - just as all other fruit in the garden.

I am most certain we make that type of logical journey in our hearts and minds daily. The Lord has given us clear-cut instructions and consequences, yet we rationalize in our minds why we can afford not to adhere to the voice of the Almighty. We feel the desire rising within; we hear the voice of the Holy Spirit within. Satan fools us into believing "we will not surely die". Maybe the Lord has instructed you to stay away from a certain person, place, thing, or idea. You can see nothing with your natural eyes that should keep you from it. That "thing" appears to be okay. Faith may not make sense in your head, but you must believe and follow with your heart. If you could see or understand it naturally, you wouldn't need faith. So is the deception of Satan. The Bible tells us that he often appears as an angel of light (2 Corinthians 11:14). Satan only comes to take, murder, and tear down. As a result, we will die - for any time we are apart from God (the source of life), death shall follow.

The Works of the Flesh

"Now the works of the flesh are manifest, which are these; adultery, fornication, uncleanness, lasciviousness, idolatry, witchcraft, hatred, variance, emulations, wrath, strife, seditions, heresies, envyings, murders, drunkenness, revellings, and such like: of the which I tell you before, as I have also told you in time past, that they which do such things shall not inherit the kingdom of God" (Galatians 5:19-21).

In Greek literature, the word 'sarx' usually meant nothing more than the human body. It was also used the same way in the New Testament (John 1:14). However, Paul often used the word to denote the entire fallen human being - not just the sinful body, but the entire being, including the soul and mind, as affected by sin. Thus, Paul often opposed the "flesh" against the "Spirit" as being two diametrically opposed forces. The works of the flesh include those, but go well beyond destructive contentions and jealousies. Where there is such behavior, it is positive proof that the person is not living in the power of the Holy Spirit, but is being energized by Satan and his hosts (Acts 5:3). The unbeliever can live only in the flesh, but the believer can live in the flesh or in the Spirit. Paul repeatedly encourages believers to overcome the deeds of the flesh by living in the Spirit.

What are the deeds of the flesh? How do I know when I'm functioning from my carnal nature? Although the 5th chapter of Galatians gives us a list of such deeds, I don't believe that passage is an all-inclusive list. It does, however, provide us with great boundaries for the Christian to live by: The scriptures help us see when we're walking in the flesh. Many of the descriptive words used by the writer of Galatians are not commonly used in our modern society. When was the last time you heard someone use the word "lasciviousness"?

To help eliminate confusion and misuse, following are all 17 words defined in their original Greek language. I pray you will discover God's great wisdom and His vast insight into the lust of the flesh.

1. **Adultery** (3430) - moicheia: the state of adultery, disloyalty, betrayal, deceitfulness, faithlessness. Often defined as unfaithfulness in marriage.
2. **Fornication** (4202) – porneia: sexual immorality, marital unfaithfulness, prostitution.
3. **Uncleanness** (167) - akatharsia: impurity, a state of moral filthiness (especially in relation to sexual sin).
4. **Lasciviousness** (766) – aselgeia: debauchery, sensuality, lewdness, filthy, wickedness, depravity.
5. **Idolatry** (1495) – eidoloatria: the reverence and worship of idols. Anyone or anything – other than the True and Living God – can become an idol.

6. **Witchcraft** (5331) - pharmakeia: magic, sorceries, the use of spells and potions of magic, often involving drugs.
7. **Hatred** (2189) - echthra: hostility, antagonism, enmity, aggression, animosity.
8. **Varience** (2054) - eris: quarrel, strife, dissension, discord, debates.
9. **Emulations** (2205) – zelos: jealousy, envy, rage, morally corrupt zealous ill will.
10. **Wrath** (2372) - thymos: fury, anger, rage, a state of intense displeasure based in some real or perceived wrong.
11. **Strife** (2052) - eritheia: selfish ambition, faction, contention.
12. **Seditions** (1370) – dichostasia: division, dissension.
13. **Heresies** (139) - hairesis: sect (religious party), faction, "clicks".
14. **Envyings** (5355) – phthonos: to be jealous of.
15. **Murders** (5408) - phonos: killing, slain, slaughter. Not only in a physical sense, but also in a mental, spiritual, and emotional sense as well.
16. **Drunkenness** (3178) – methe: to get drunk, intoxicated.
17. **Revellings** (2970) – komos: carousing, rioting.

Jesus' Temptation – Israel's Wilderness

"And the devil said unto Him, "If thou be the Son of God, command this stone that it be made bread"" (Luke 4:3).

Christ had gone many weeks without eating and was obviously very hungry. Satan, therefore, used Jesus' natural desire for food to suggest that He should use His supernatural powers to create food and eat it. This type of temptation can be very difficult because it fights against our very nature of self-preservation. Jesus knew that food was necessary for a person's physical needs, but He also knew that obedience to the Father was far more important. Seeing that God initiated the fast, God alone would decide when and how His fast would end.

Is that not mankind's trouble? We are tempted to fulfill and supply our physical needs. If God takes care of the flowers of the field and the birds in the trees, surely He loves us enough to supply our every need as well. Our powers are limited; therefore, our abilities to satisfy our carnal cravings are limited as well. Our powers and abilities are temporary; therefore, our capacity to satisfy is temporary as well.

"And Jesus answered him, saying, "It is written, that man shall not live by bread alone, but by every Word of God"" (Luke 4:4).

"And he humbled thee, and suffered thee to hunger, and fed thee with manna, which thou knewest not, neither did thy fathers know; that he might make thee know that man doth not live by bread only, but by every word that proceedeth out of the mouth of the LORD doth man live" (Deuteronomy 8:3).

The varied experiences of life in the wilderness taught Israel that life depends on more than the food people eat and the water they drink. It depends upon spiritual forces that are found only in God. The Israelites were to keep this in mind when they settled in Canaan, a land they would find to be rich in natural resources. They were to fear God and thank Him for His gifts.

Every day, I see the efforts of countless single and married men and women striving to fulfill their physical cravings by their own methods. Whether starving for attention, affection, comfort, or even finances, we make a grave mistake without the Lord being involved in our efforts. Many women are heartbroken repeatedly, searching for a man to love them. A great number of men spend everything they have, attempting to buy respect, promotion, and appreciation. Countless men and women will do anything to fulfill the longing hunger and desire that lies within their soul.

Amazingly, all our needs - even physical ones - can be met only in the presence of the Lord. It was only in His presence that the Israelites were fully satisfied; it is only in His presence that we will be abundantly satisfied as well.

Everyday Jesus

"In the meanwhile, His disciples prayed to Him saying, "Master, eat." But He said unto them, "I have meat to eat that ye know not of." Therefore said the disciples one to another, "Hath any man brought Him ought to eat?" Jesus saith unto them, "My meat is to do the will of Him that sent me, and to finish His work. Say not ye, "There are yet four months, and then cometh harvest?" Behold, I say unto you, "Lift up your eyes, and look on the fields; for they are white already to harvest"" (John 4:31-35).

Physical food is very necessary to sustain our physical being (it's the way God designed us), but it is not the only thing we need to sustain life. We live by every Word that comes from the mouth of God (Matthew 4:4). The grass withers, the flowers fade, but the Word of God stands forever (Isaiah 40:8).

As a result, for Jesus, it was necessary (meat) to do the will of God. It was in fulfilling the Word of God that Jesus sustained His very life. This food does not simply know the will of God, but does it as well. It is practice or output (Hebrews 5:12-14) that brings forth the fulfillment of God's promises in our lives. It is not just enough to know the will of God; we must be doers as well - not just hearers only. The devil and his demons know there is One True and Living God, but they lack what is necessary to perform the work of the Lord.

It is your faith that must propel you past knowledge into complete engagement (James 2:19-20). Far too often, we stop with input rather than going on to output or productivity. Jesus, being our loving and giving Lord, wished to share His 'meat' with His followers. Jesus offered His disciples an opportunity to do something that would be "food" for them. He was speaking directly about the Samaritans. *"Open your spiritual eyes and you will be able to see that a great harvest lies before you."* In them, He saw an opportunity for a spiritual harvest for which they would not have to wait long.

In like-fashion, I implore you to "open" your spiritual eyes. There is plenty of work for you to do. You can be completely and permanently satisfied by doing the will of our Lord.

My Personal Walk

It can be very difficult to speak openly and honestly about the lust of my flesh. A great sense of horror and shame overwhelms me just to think about them. *What if someone discovered the deep dark secrets that I purposely hide from the outside world? If I dislike this sin that is with me, I can only imagine what the Lord feels.* Those heart-gripping emotions, at times, have captivated my every waking thought. Therefore, over the course of time, I have pushed those issues as far from the light as possible - hoping, wishing, and even praying that no one ever discovered the truth.

As much as we love the dark, the funny thing is that help can only be found in the light. In the midst of my great fear, the Lord still spoke to me: *"What if someone can learn from the failures of your life? As hopeless as it may seem, I can still get glory from your life."* So, I press on to expose the truth, praying that someone is helped in the process. Although the lust of my eyes and the pride of life have had the most disastrous effects on me, the lust of the flesh had been the greatest challenge for me to overcome. This is probably true because the lust of my flesh was enjoyed the most. If we would be honest, we would rarely indulge in sin if it was not enjoyable...

Drugs and alcohol had their place in my past. Overeating was relatively easy to conquer, but wrong views and feelings toward sex have been my stronghold for what seems to be forever. It started early in life as a preadolescent. While going through that change in life, I was not taught the biblical view of sex. There were no talks about sex. There were no talks about choices and consequences. There were no talks of what to and what not to do. All I was told was, "Don't do it until you get married." But why? That reasoning may work for a child, but it certainly doesn't hold much water with a young adult. I had so many raging hormones coursing through my body and no idea how to rightfully deal with them. Because I did not understand the consequences of sexual sin, I began to "taste" and "dabble" into things that would haunt me to this day. Because I did not possess a biblical view of sexual relationships, I had little choice but to have a worldly view.

This is a great time to encourage parents to talk to their children about sex. Yes, it may be uncomfortable, but it is your duty as a parent. If you don't teach your child [Godly and biblical principles), who will teach them? Trust me; Satan is going to do his job! He will be certain to teach your child every evil that he possibly can.

Very early in life - maybe the 7th grade - I began to view pornography. It started as soft-core pornography (magazines, videos, internet) and grew into the physical act of depicting all that I had seen. Because of self-esteem issues (this will be discussed later), masturbation was the quickest and easiest way to fulfill those sexual desires. That seemingly harmless "pet" grew into an almost uncontrollable "beast". The desire that grew within me became so great that, at times, I would perform sexual acts virtually any and everywhere. It was a spirit that would come over me. It would take control of me. Almost any place at any time, I would have to satisfy that physical desire - with myself, my girlfriend, a stranger…it didn't matter. At the end of the day, as long as I was fulfilled and satisfied, nothing else really mattered.

The deceptiveness of Satan is to make one believe they are truly satisfied. The problem with allowing Satan to satisfy you is the happiness (fulfillment) will only last for a short period of time - and just like with any drug, you need more the next time to achieve the same high. So each time, I would want more, desire more, crave more, and need more. Then one day, you look up and you're performing, viewing, and saying things you never could have imagined would be a reality.

Then there came the joyous day I met Jesus. He paid my sin debt and washed my sins away. Through His redemptive work, I was now a new creature; old things were passed away, all things were now new. Still, that "old man" would soon be resurrected…by none other than me. Soon after, the accursed sexual life I lived before salvation would creep back into my regenerated life. This time, I had help to conquer and kill the "beast" that lived within. My help would come from the great Holy Spirit of God!

I cannot say that I no longer have issues. I still do from time to time. What I do know is this: Every day I continue to press past my sins and into the presence of Almighty God. While in His presence, He can rebuke me, correct me, instruct me, and love me back to Him.

Discovering how I should think about sex has been a great learning process. It may be comical, but it is true. Like G.I. Joe, now I know…and knowing is half the battle!

Our Solution

"This I say then: Walk in the Spirit, and ye shall not fulfil the lust of the flesh. For the flesh lustesth against the Spirit, and the Spirit against the flesh: and these are contrary the one to the other: so that ye cannot do the things ye would. And they that are Christ's have crucified the flesh with the affections and lusts. If we live in the Spirit, let us also walk in the Spirit" (Galatians 5:16-17, 24-25).

When the Apostle Paul instructs us to "walk", he is actually telling us to live in the Spirit. His command was that we should conduct our lives as people being influenced and overshadowed by God's Holy Spirit. The only consistent way to overcome the sinful desires of our human nature is to live step-by-step in the power of the Holy Spirit as He works through our spirit.

I won't lie to you, though: It isn't easy.

When I think of my life, this physical being is what I've always known. God is a Spirit; therefore, I cannot see Him with my physical eyes. At times, it becomes very easy to lose focus of who He is. It can be very difficult to focus on the Lord when the object of our desire and lust is right before us. The troubles of life almost force us to look at the physical instead of the spiritual (Matthew 14:29-31).

God is a Spirit - but I can see my bills.

God is a Spirit - but I can see my hurting loved-one.

God is a Spirit - but I can feel the longing dissatisfaction deep within my heart.

The Word of God declares that God is a Spirit, and those who worship Him must do so in spirit and in truth.

Christians are spiritually "crucified". They are no longer subjected (slaves) to the values or desires of the world. However, it remains difficult for Christians to apply this spiritual reality to the passions of the flesh. Those who have mastered those sinful desires are those who have kept their focus on the Messiah. Through prayer, meditation, worship, and the reading of God's Word, we keep our focus on things that are above (eternal things). I have found the more I obey the Holy Spirit, the easier it becomes. Jesus tells us that if we love Him, we will possess a heart of obedience.

Too often, I've stopped to argue with Lord. To think, this "little one" would have the nerve to argue with the Most High, the Maker of Heaven and Earth. Even now, I wonder: *Why argue? Why struggle? Why fight against the promptings of the Holy Spirit?* What God wants for us is only good, never bad; but it is my flesh that continues to disappoint me day by day. Life is much easier when I obey God's voice. Sure, I sometimes miss my carnal desires, but they are usually the very things I don't need. To give up what I don't need in order to gain what I am truly in need of is a small price to pay. As well, God never asks us to give up anything without returning to us greater and immeasurably beyond what we sacrificed.

In the letter to the Galatians, Paul exhorts them to walk in the Spirit because they are already living in the Spirit. This type of walk is to follow, to adhere, and to listen to the encouragements of the Holy Spirit. To keep this definition simple, it plainly means to obey. Such an action should be natural, but unfortunately, we are at war with our fallen nature. To "walk in the Spirit" means to obey the promptings of the Holy Spirit. There is no second-guessing, room for hesitation, or even moments of procrastination. When God speaks to our spirits, we must respond promptly with a heart that says "YES!" That type of response is only generated through a living and active relationship with our Creator.

The Word declares, *"My sheep hear and know my voice…and the voice of a stranger they will not follow"* (John 10:4-5). So often, we are distracted and easily swayed because we have not spent the quality time necessary to hear and discern the voice of God.

"I am crucified with Christ: nevertheless, I live; yet not I, but Christ liveth in me: and the life which I now live in the flesh I live by the faith of the Son of God, who loved me, and gave Himself for me" (Galatians 2:20).

When you are not following your fleshly urges to walk at your own pace, you feel the direct guidance of the Holy Spirit step-by-step along the way. When you are walking in harmony with the Spirit, the fruit of your relationship with Him is evident. When you keep in step with Him, He keeps your feet on His good path. In order for that to take place, one must come to the "end" of himself. In order for that to happen, one must be a broken vessel in the hands of the Lord.

The tears I've cried through the "breaking" process are countless. Not always knowing why I had to endure such heartache, I now know the Lord was breaking me to make me into a new and better vessel. Today, looking back on the journey, I am a better servant of Christ for it. I thank God for the painful - but necessary - pruning in my life (Hebrews 12:11). Therefore, it was good that I was afflicted. Because of my afflictions, I was able to learn the ways of the Lord. I was able to become more intimately acquainted with Him. Because of the hard times, I am now able to better walk in a manner that is pleasing to Jesus Christ (Psalm 119:71).

Closing Thought

"He who avoids the temptation avoids the sin."
~ Author Unknown

My 2nd Love Letter to God

(Use this section to be honest with both God and yourself. Tell God why you LOVE HIM, what you need forgiveness for, and why you are grateful.)

THE LUST OF THE EYES

"For all that is in the world … the lust of the eyes … is not of the Father, but is of the world" (1 John 2:16).

"At the core of most problems is a truth that is being denied."
~ The 4th Secret of the One Minute Manager

Our lustful eyes, our evil thoughts, and our vain imaginations make up the lust of the eyes. This can also include what we hear and what we think or meditate upon in our minds. In popular culture, much is said about the eyes of man. "The hand is quicker than the eye" is the first one that comes to my mind. That statement leads us to believe we cannot always trust or fully embrace that which we perceive with our physical eyes. Therefore, the Scriptures tell us to operate by faith - not by what outside circumstances dictate.

Through the years, I have realized that my "eyes" contribute greatly to the wants of my sinful flesh. Have you ever watched a television commercial and noticed soon after that you desired the very product or service advertised? For example, you see a hamburger commercial and the next moment...you desire a hamburger! It's not that you are necessarily hungry, but your senses have been tickled to imagine what 'could be'. *"I could get a hamburger. I sure could use a good hamburger! In fact, what's to stop me from getting a hamburger?"* I believe this to be a great problem in our American society. The movies, internet, magazines, videos, and so much more, all point us away from God. Most of the vices steer us towards sex, drugs, violence, and laziness.

As Scripture says, *"For as he thinketh in his heart, so is he..."* (Proverbs 23:7). What we physically look at and listen to will play a great role in our progressive thought-life. Scripture also tells us that our thoughts determine who we are (for it is our thoughts that control what we do). Therefore, it has always been a challenge for mankind to change the input in order to redirect the output.

David's Wandering Eyes

King David's magnificent triumphs and sorrowful defeats are recorded in the Book of 2nd Samuel. From his complicated rise to the throne to his famous last words, his biography describes a remarkable and divinely-inspired leader. Countless individuals have looked to him as an example of leadership. King David took a divided and miserably-defeated Israel from his predecessor, King Saul, and built a prominent nation. Like most political biographies, 2nd Samuel highlights the good character traits that enabled David to succeed:

- His reliance on God for guidance (2:1);
- His genuineness (5:1-5); and
- His courage (5:6-7).

The book also describes the tragic consequences of David's lust (12:1-23) and destructive pride (24:1-17). By presenting both the strengths and weaknesses of David, the book gives a complete picture of a very real person - a person from whom we can learn a great deal.

"And it came to pass in an eveningtide, that David arose from off his bed, and walked upon the roof of the king's house: and from the roof he saw a woman washing herself; and the woman was very beautiful to look upon. And David sent and enquired after the woman. And one said, "Is not this Bathsheba, the daughter of Eliam, the wife of Uriah the Hittite?" And David sent messengers, and took her; and she came in unto him, and he lay with her; for she was purified from her uncleanness: and she returned unto her house" (2 Samuel 11:2-4).

During that time in David's life, he committed a series of sins that brought him much sorrow and trouble for the rest of his life. We must be exceedingly mindful that our actions do not only carry temporary results; they also hold a far greater weight throughout all eternity.

If you will read 2 Samuel 11:1, you will see that it was wartime. What was David doing at home during a time of war? Success often causes complacency, and we find ourselves in the wrong place at the wrong time. If David would have been on the battlefield, he could have avoided much grief and sorrow. After David laid with Bathsheba (wife of Uriah, one of David's top soldiers), he was guilty of sexual immorality. What an insurmountable level of betrayal of loyalty and trust to one who would have died to save the king's life! David then tried to disgracefully cover his mistakes by means of murder…but none of his tactics worked. If we look closely, we will see that David's problems started when his eyes left the Lord and became transfixed on Bathsheba. Scripture says that Bathsheba was **very** beautiful. Rarely does Scripture describe the physical appearance of people, but both David (1 Samuel 16:12) and Bathsheba are described as being of exceptionally-fine appearance. Therefore, like the forbidden fruit, David would also be subdued partly by the lust of his eyes.

The lust of the eyes subtly and artfully draws us away from the Word of God and devours our confidence in Him. We see what the world has to offer and desire it above our relationship with God. We begin to place more credence in our own perspective of life than in God's faithful commands and blessed promises. Fueled by the lust for what we see, we frantically seize all we can get, believing we must have it. At the same time, we are terribly deceived, believing God wants us to have it. Wrongly assuming that God will withhold nothing good from us, we lustfully claim we have achieved prosperity.

The eyes (spiritually and physically) must be very important. They are mentioned over 478 times throughout the Old and New Testaments. In Deuteronomy 29:4, the Bible speaks of individuals having no eyes to perceive spiritual matters. In Proverbs 16:2 and 27:20, the Lord speaks of mankind's eyes never being satisfied and how we believe we are correct in all that we do. In Psalm 199:18, David prayed an honest prayer for his eyes to be opened. That is something every believer needs to confess before the throne of God: ***"Open my eyes that I may see!"*** It is not something you can do on your own. The carnal man does not understand or perceive spiritual things. It is only through the grace and will of God that we are able to see life through the eyes of God. Even still, it is only through the grace and will of God that we are able to change our lives and align ourselves (mind, body, and soul) with the views of the Lord.

Herod's Lustful Eyes

The Gospel of Matthew has many Jewish overtones. No other Gospel lays such stress on the kingdom. The Jewish people patiently longed for the restoration of the glorious kingdom of King David. That hunger was a burning hope for many Jews at the time. Matthew clearly identifies Jesus with that hope by using the Jewish royal title "Son of David" nine times in his Gospel. The Gospel of Matthew helps our modern culture understand the time and place of Jesus. It allows us to not only look at spiritual principles; we can also appreciate political issues as well.

"For Herod had laid hold on John, and bound him, and put him in prison for Herodias' sake, his brother Philip's wife. For John said unto him, "It is not lawful for thee to have her." And when he would have put him to death, he feared the multitude, because they counted him as a prophet. But when Herod's birthday was kept, the daughter of Herodias danced before them, and pleased Herod. Whereupon he promised with an oath to give her whatsoever she would ask. And she, being before instructed of her mother, said, "Give me here John Baptist's head in a charger." And the king was sorry: nevertheless, for the oath's sake, and them which sat with him at meat, he commanded it to be given her. And he sent, and beheaded John in the prison" (Matthew 14:3-10).

Herod is the name of several Roman rulers in Palestine during New Testament times. The Herod mentioned in the above Scritpures is Herod Antipas, who ruled from 4 B.C. to 39 A.D. He is the Herod who Jesus called a "fox" (Luke 13:32). He is also the same Herod who returned Jesus for sentencing by Pilate (Luke 23:6-12). In the above cited Scriptures, the beautiful woman (Herodias) danced so gracefully, it completely captivated Herod. Her dancing enticed his mind to dream and fantasize about all the lustful possibilities. As his eye gave place for his imagination, something almost "magical" began to happen within Herod: Herodias' dance placed Herod in such a daze, he was willing to do anything to please her. He was actually willing to give half of his kingdom for that most pleasurable "strip tease".

That same type of overwhelming haze can be seen on the faces of millions as they watch television, listen to the radio, or ponder the evil deeds they would love to commit.

In the Beginning - Pleasant to the Eyes

"And when the woman saw that the tree was ... pleasant to the eyes..." (Genesis 3:6).

Before sin entered the world, man enjoyed unbroken fellowship with the Lord. In the Book of Genesis, we read that God would come to Adam, walking in the cool of the day. There was a natural flow of sweet fellowship between God and man. There was no hint of discontentment or emerging pressure; just loving fellowship. We have no idea how great that type of fellowship is for our souls. However, that all came to an abrupt end when man disobeyed God by eating of the Tree of Knowledge. The lust of the eyes was fraudulently instrumental in the fall of man. Today, the same lust still lures us into great temptation.

The fruit on the Tree of Knowledge was pleasant to the eyes. It was a beautiful color and very inviting. The fruit exuded loveliness, vitality, and health. Therefore, at that moment, what Eve perceived with her eyes outweighed what she knew in her heart to be true (Genesis 3:2-3). I believe if man could have taken his "eyes" off of the fruit, he could have resisted temptation. He needed to change his physical eyes and his mental thoughts toward the fruit. The longer he looked at the fruit, the greater his desire became for it, while at the same time, the weaker his will became to obey his Creator.

Jesus' Temptation – Israel's Wilderness

It was said by both Matthew and Luke that Jesus was shown all the superb kingdoms of the world. Clearly, that was an empty attempt by Satan to play on the visual senses of Almighty Jesus. That wonderful showing tempted the natural eyes of Jesus, just as the luscious fruit tempted Eve in the Garden of Eden. Not only was Jesus shown the kingdoms of the world, but all of their glory as well. He was shown all of their resources as well as all of their magnificence. Jesus was shown their cities, great lands, brilliant people, massive armies, shining treasures, gorgeous temples, and more.

Is this not what Satan cleverly does to us? He shows us something with our eyes which, in turn, excites our imagination. He gets our minds to wonder. Satan continually offers us an invitation to our fallen imagination. More times than not, we follow the very thing that looks good to our eyes. We follow the very thing that is forbidden. Just think: Of all the hundreds of trees in the Garden that could have been eaten from, mankind desired the one thing that was completely off-limits.

One of the reasons Jesus came to live among us was to personally identify with our carnal needs and our human struggles. For that reason, He understands exactly how we feel under the crushing weight of temptation. He has faced the tempter – and He has overcome the darkness and adversity associated with Satan's fiery trials.

"And Jesus answered and said unto him, "Get thee behind me, Satan: for it is written, "Thou shalt worship the Lord thy God, and Him only shalt thou serve"" (Luke 4:8).

"Thou shalt fear the LORD thy God, and serve Him, and shalt swear by His name" (Deuteronomy 6:13).

Yahweh is the only God - the One Living God. He loved Israel as His specially-chosen people, and He wanted them to love Him in return. God, on His part, would feel excruciating pain and sorrowful grief if, in their prosperity, they forgot Him or if they turned away from Him to follow idol gods. The people, on their part, would find full satisfaction through walking humbly before their God and keeping His law.

The nation of Israel, however, grieved God's heart continually by repeatedly chasing after other gods and withholding their loving devotion and sincere adoration from Him. Today, God longs for the same intimate relationship with you. He would do anything - and has done everything - to receive your love (John 3:16). In the most radical display of all time, He provided His Son, Jesus Christ, as the means to make such unconditional fellowship possible.

God is and evermore shall be the passionate and faithful Lover of your soul.

Everyday Jesus

"Now when He came nigh to the gate of the city, behold, there was a dead man carried out, the only son of his mother, and she was a widow: and much people of the city was with her. And when the Lord saw her, He had compassion on her, and said unto her, "Weep not"" (Luke 7:12-13).

In the northern town of Nain, the Chosen One [Jesus] (Luke 9:35) is seen amazingly raising a widow's son to new life. It seems that in this case, He acted not because of any heartfelt request, but solely because of the tender sympathy He felt for the widow. That was nothing new for Jesus. Sorrow and need have always touched His loving heart. Oftentimes, love and pity are mentioned as motives for Christ's miracles (i.e. Matthew 14:14; Matthew 15:32). With her husband and her only son dead, the widow was faced with tumultuous hardship and depressing poverty for the rest of her natural life.

Our Life (Colossians 3:4) stopped the funeral procession and gave the woman 's son regenerated life. Take notice here of the genuine motivation of Jesus' heart. He was not moved by egotistical greed, lust, power, or pride. The Scripture says He looked on her with compassion. Far too often, we look at individuals with evil motives and wicked intentions - but not Jesus! Everything He says and every act He does flows out of care and empathetic concern for His people. Therefore, as His disciples, we must look at the people and circumstances in our lives with great sympathy, overflowing concern, and genuine care.

"And if thine eye offend thee, pluck it out, and cast it from thee: it is better for thee to enter into life with one eye, rather than having two eyes to be cast into hell fire" (Matthew 18:9).

In that passage of Scripture, Jesus is not teaching us to dismember our physical bodies. Rather, He is instructing us in this manner: If the most cherished enjoyment or the most adored and helpful person turns you away from serving Christ or hinders your Christian walk, it should be done away with. That is what the Scriptures mean when it tells us to "hate our mother". As much as you may love your mother, father, sister, or brother, they cannot come before the Lord. If they do, they must be done away with and put in proper perspective.

The disciples had been told that there would be seducers, tempters, persecutors, and bad examples. Thus, they were to be on a constant spiritual guard. We must - as much as we are able - part with what we cannot keep without being entangled by it in sin. The outward occasions of sin must be avoided.

How many television shows do we watch that draw us into thinking erroneous thoughts?

How many magazines do we thumb through in hopes of seeing something that would satisfy our lustful eyes?

How many times do we turn around to take a second look at the opposite sex as they (unknowingly) waltz into the distance?

Pluck it out.

Separate yourself.

Do away with it.

If the "eye candy" of this world keeps tripping you up,
get rid of it!

My Personal Walk

As stated earlier, the lust of the eyes includes our evil thoughts and imaginations. Those thoughts are largely influenced by what we see and hear; therefore, I include sight and sound in this category.

At the onset, the lusts of my eyes were largely promoted by what I watched on television. There was a time not so long ago when a person could watch television without fear of being bombarded by images and expressions of violence, drugs, sex, and inappropriate language. That former time was followed by an era where very few channels could be watched with a level of Christian-approval (usually our non-cable channels). Now, however, the day has arrived when the whole television set must be "thrown" at the feet of Jesus!

Violence, drugs, and the pull towards instant monetary gratification did not appeal to me very much. My hang-up with television was primarily comedy. Anyone who knows me realizes I am a very animated and comical individual. As with any God-given character trait, it has its place and has often come in handy. *"After all, it's all just innocent fun! Who doesn't enjoy a good laugh? By the way, who is it hurting?"* With those thoughts guiding me, I traveled deeper into a pit of self-destruction. I grew up with that being a normal part of life, not realizing that I am the one being hurt. The jokes became meaner…and darker. The gags became crueler. The funny stories grew worse and worse. Before I knew it, I found myself laughing at jokes being made about my Lord and Savior Jesus Christ!

The television show portrayed Him in activity that should make all of mankind repent. It was not enough that they had what we consider 'His earthly likeness'; the show actually used His name! Like David, I should've been appalled and horrified that someone would dare mock the True and Living God - but I wasn't upset in the least. In fact, I was amused. This all pointed to a much deeper spiritual issue. Then, there came that atoning moment when the Holy Spirit touched me. At that moment, my eyes were opened. *"What are you laughing at?"* He said to me. *"What is so funny about the Savior of your soul being depicted in this manner?"* I then realized: I had a problem.

It might be alright if it stopped there, but our input always determines our output. So, all of that trash I was so happily consuming would soon come back to bite me. I found myself saying and thinking things contrary to God's will. I found myself hurting people with my words - for my amusement. I found myself becoming what I saw and heard around me. You are what you eat, much like whatever you watch and listen to, you shall soon become.

Once again, the joys of knowing Jesus delivered me. Although I was already saved, knowing Christ is a never-ending process. As we grow to know Him, we grow to know what is acceptable in His sight. Therefore, the Lord has patiently worked with me to change what I watch and listen to. The more I dwell on the things of God, the better my thoughts and words become. The Psalmist says to hide God's Word in our hearts to prevent us from sinning. The only true way to put God's Word in your heart is through continually dwelling in His presence - and regularly studying the Bible.

Through the years, my love for being with God and my love for studying His Word has grown. That is the only true way I have been able to overcome in this area. Instead of submersing myself in the things of this world, I completely submerse myself in the Word and Spirit of God.

Our Solution

"I made a covenant with mine eyes; why then should I think upon a maid?" (Job 31:1).

"But I say unto you, that whosoever looketh on a woman to lust after her hath committed adultery with her already in his heart" (Matthew 5:28).

A man or woman who gazes upon another with the purpose of wanting them sexually has mentally and in their heart committed adultery. Like murder, adultery is the final fruit of wrong thoughts and uncontrolled feelings. The eyes see, the mind desires, and the body reacts. Therefore, the eye - as well as the rest of the body - must be brought under control, whatever the cost. That is why Job made an agreement with his eyes that he would not lust after another woman. Temptation must be cut off at the source: the inward man.

We must be careful of the company we keep, the books we read, the television programs we watch, and so much more. All of those things will adversely affect what our eyes gravitate towards. If our eyes are looking, our minds are thinking. All of those things desire to find a resting place within our hearts. If you are viewing pornography, it will eventually find a resting place in your heart and become a part of you. If you are watching excessively violent behavior, you, too, will become excessively violent. If you are "innocently" looking at any ungodly activity, it shall soon become a part of who you are.

"Lust not after her beauty in thine heart; neither let her take thee with her eyelids. For by means of a whorish woman a man is brought to a piece of bread: and the adulteress will hunt for the precious life. Can a man take fire in his bosom, and his clothes not be burned? Can one go upon hot coals, and his feet not be burned? So he that goeth in to his neighbor's wife; whosoever toucheth her shall not be innocent" (Proverbs 6:25-29).

When you face temptation, know that you do not face it alone: Jesus is with you. He provides the strength you need to say "no" to every dark thought or evil imagination. In times of temptation, when the enemy reveals images of woe-some doubt and discouragement, take your stand against him by clothing yourself in the mighty armor of God (Ephesians 6). Also know that being tempted is not a sin. All are tempted. Even Jesus was tempted (Luke 4:1-13). Therefore, temptation is not a sin. Sin is the result of acting on the temptation. No matter how weak you may feel, God always provides the strength you need to steer clear of temptation. You can say "no" to all evil because Jesus lives in you. He has given you the Holy Spirit to lead you into all knowledge and truth. Child of God, take your stand! Claim His strength and victory!

One tool I have used to control and eliminate lustful thoughts and imaginations is changing what I listen to and watch on television. Each morning, I recite particular scriptures over my family and myself. As I ride in the car, I listen to the praises of the Lord through song. In the evening, instead of watching television, I read and study my Bible. All of those things may seem small and minimal. However, when done collectively five days a week, they have had a great impact on strengthening my spirit-man. You should try it! I am a witness: It works!

Closing Thought

"Moral failure is rarely the result of a blowout;
almost always, it's the result of a slow leak."
~ Gary Oliver

My 3rd Love Letter to God

(Use this section to be honest with both God and yourself. Tell God why you LOVE HIM, what you need forgiveness for, and why you are grateful.)

THE PRIDE OF LIFE

"For all that is in the world … the pride of life, is not of the Father, but is of the world" (1 John 2:16).

"People with humility don't think less of themselves. They just think about themselves less."

~ The 4th Secret of the One Minute Manager

Probably one of the most deadening of the three, the Pride of Life can easily be seen as we look at the Book of 2 Chronicles. The Pride of Life consists of arrogance and boasting in self. As the Apostle Paul expresses it, *"Thinking more highly about oneself than he should"* (Romans 12:3). As detrimental as pride is, it can be very subtle and cunning.

I must confess: Pride was and is one of my greatest battles. Growing up, I possessed such a low self-image. I always viewed myself as a nerd, a geek, and a social castaway. I saw myself as someone that no one desired. God had to perform a mighty work to bring me from the fringes of self-loathing and depression. Once renewed and restored, my outlook and self-image shifted to the opposite end of the spectrum: pride. What my Father desired for me the whole time was humility - the polar opposite of pride.

Biblical humility is grounded in the character of God.

- The Father stoops down to help the poor and needy (Psalm 113:4-9); and
- The incarnate Son exhibits humility from the manger to the cross (Matthew 11:29).

The dual usage of "meek" and "humble in heart" emphasizes Christ's humility before humankind - those whom He came to serve and His submission before God. We must remember that humility and meekness are often inseparable (Colossians 3:12).

Most people understand that pride consists of feelings of superiority about self. On the opposite end of the spectrum, pride also includes those who think too low of themselves. In the Greek language, pride is defined as 'insolent and empty assurance'. That empty assurance trusts in its own power and resources; it shamefully despises and violates God's laws. Thinking too little of yourself is essentially not agreeing with God. That type of pride says, "Lord, you don't know what you're talking about. I'm less than what you have called me to be". Our loving Father continues to reassure us that we are created in His image. Do we agree with that? No. Feelings of resentment and unworthiness drive us deeper into the pit of despair, instead of driving us into the loving arms of Jesus.

For it is the Lord who declares, "Cast your cares on Me, for I care for you". Therefore, pride is much more than haughtiness and arrogance. Pride is possessing an attitude and self-image that does not line up with God's attitude and views.

King Saul's Mess

In the Book of 1st Samuel, King Saul's extraordinary rise to power and influence - and his subsequent tragic fall - are recounted. In a sense, the book reads like a classic Greek tragedy. Saul's good looks, physical size, and success in war made him an obvious choice to become the first king of Israel. Still, the author of 1st Samuel highlights Saul's tragic flaw: his disobedience to God's commandments. His disobedience led to God's rejection of him. Abandoned by God, Saul quickly lost his courage, became jealous of David's success, and eventually lost his mind. It's a very sad story, but one we can learn from nonetheless.

"And when Samuel rose early to meet Saul in the morning, it was told Samuel, saying, "Saul came to Carmel, and, behold, he set him up a place, and is gone about, and passed on, and gone down to Gilgal." And Samuel came to Saul: and Saul said unto him, "Blessed be thou of the LORD: I have performed the commandment of the LORD." And Samuel said, "What meaneth then this bleating of the sheep in mine ears, and the lowing of the oxen which I hear?" And Saul said, "They have brought them from the Amalekites: for the people spared the best of the sheep and of the oxen, to sacrifice unto the LORD thy God; and the rest we have utterly destroyed." Then Samuel said unto Saul, "Stay, and I will tell thee what the LORD hath said to me on this night." And he said unto him, "Say on." And Samuel said, "When thou wast little in thine own sight, wast thou not made the head of the tribes of Israel, and the LORD anointed thee king over Israel? And the LORD sent thee on a journey, and said, "Go and utterly destroy the sinners the Amalekites, and fight against them until they be consumed." Wherefore, then, didst thou not obey the voice of the LORD, but didst fly upon the spoil, and didst evil in the sight of the LORD?"" (1 Samuel 15:12-19).

King Saul has just messed up. He messed up big! The higher the Lord elevates us, the greater the responsibility (Luke 12:48). If you continue reading future chapters, Saul repeatedly messes up until his death. At that point, God had given him clear-cut instructions, but did he follow them? Not exactly. Delayed obedience is not obedience. Partial obedience is not obedience. Our God requires full obedience. It is prideful to think we know more than God. Surely, no one would say, "I know more than God". When we 'twist' God's instructions, we say, "God, your way is good - but my way is just a little bit better".

King Uzziah's Destruction

When it was first written, 2nd Chronicles brought a ray of hope to a people desperately in need of encouragement. The Israelite community had been reduced to a tiny minority in exile among the Babylonians, and they were struggling to understand their place. Had God's promises to Abraham and David been revoked because of the nation's sins? Was there any hope of reviving David's dynasty? Could Judaism survive without the temple? 2nd Chronicles addressed questions like those. Its answers came in a historical review of God's faithfulness to the Israelites. Although the nation had steadily declined over the centuries, the Holy One had always been faithful to those who remained true to Him. The good that God had done in the past would be the pattern for His future acts. God would keep His glorious promises to the Israelites.

"And he made in Jerusalem engines, invented by cunning men, to be on the towers and upon the bulwarks, to shoot arrows and great stones withal. And his name spread far abroad; for he was marvellously helped, till he was strong. But when he was strong, his heart was lifted up to his destruction: for he transgressed against the LORD his God, and went into the temple of the LORD to burn incense upon the altar of incense" (2 Chronicles 26:15-16).

Under the rule of Uzziah (or Azariah), the kingdom of Judah enjoyed remarkable growth and tremendous prosperity. Many marvelous inventions and wonderful works were manifested as long as Uzziah humbly followed God. Unfortunately, that God-given success made Uzziah proud, and he arrogantly took to himself the rights of a priest. The writer points out that although the priesthood and the kingship were both appointed by God, they were separate and independent systems. One could not take over the functions of the other.

In God, you come up against something which is in every respect immeasurably superior to yourself. Unless you know God as that - and, therefore, know yourself as nothing in comparison - you do not know God at all. As long as you are proud, you cannot know God. A proud man is always looking down on things and people and, of course, as long as you are looking down, you cannot see something that is above you (i.e. our Heavenly Father).

Many proverbs contrast the arrogant with the humble.

- "Pride goeth before destruction and an haughty spirit before a fall" (Proverbs 16:18).
- "God hath sworn to lift on high who sinks himself by true humility" (John Keble).
- "Seest thou a man wise in his own conceit? There is more hope of a fool than of him" (Proverbs 26:12).
- "Lowliness is the base of every virtue, and he who does the lowest builds the fastest" (Philip James Bailey).
- "Be of the same mind one toward another. Mind not high things, but condescend to men of low estate. Be not wise in your own conceits" (Romans 12:17).
- "O, be very sure that no man will learn anything at all, unless he first learn humility" (Lord Lytton).

The Hebrew word for pride comes from a root that means "to boil up"; it refers to a raging arrogance or stubborn insolence. The image pictures the presumptions or arrogant behavior of the godless person. That type of behavior always leads to regretful shame - shame from others and shame for ourselves, for pride always precedes a great fall (Proverbs 16:18). The word 'pride' (as we are studying it) does not refer to self-esteem or to a positive mental attitude, but to arrogance and a refusal to glorify God. Such pride is self-serving and always leads to conflict.

In the Beginning – Desirable to Make One Wise

"And when the woman saw that the tree was good … desired to make one wise…" (Genesis 3:6).

Pride was, above all else, the most engaging and prevailing motive to influence Eve to eat of the tree. She possessed an eager desire for more wisdom and knowledge. Her desire to be more like God was truly a satanic deception, for in her pure, sinless state, she was as close to being like the Lord as humanly possible.

Every day, in our efforts and feelings of superiority, we make ourselves less like God – instead of conforming to His express image. Far too often, we believe we know something, when in fact, we know nothing. We believe we have obtained something, when we have actually lost everything. The Apostle Paul counted everything he knew as nothing compared to the knowledge of Christ (Philippians 3:8). We must do the same as Paul, allowing nothing to separate us from the love of Christ. The virtue opposite to pride (in Christian morals) is called humility. The utmost evil is called pride. Murder, anger, greed, and drunkenness are all mere fleabites in comparison. It is through pride that Lucifer became Satan. Pride leads to every other intolerable vice. It is the complete anti-God state of mind.

"How art thou fallen from Heaven, O Lucifer, son of the morning! How are thou cut down to the ground, which didst weaken the nations! For thou hast said in thine heart, "I will ascend into Heaven, I will exalt my throne above the stars of God: I will sit also upon the mount of the congregation, in the sides of the North: I will ascend above the heights of the clouds; I will be like the most High"" (Isaiah 14:12-14).

No matter how it is displayed, pride (like all other sins) is a choice. The very fall of Satan was caused by the tricky indulgence known as pride. He is the one who chose to think, feel, and act in the manner he did and continues to do this day. It was Satan who said to himself, *"I'll climb to the top of the clouds. I'll take over as King of the Universe!"* God, however, would triumphantly proclaim, **"Not so, Lucifer!"** At that moment, Satan was cast out of Heaven and became what we know him to be today (1 Peter 5:8). Even now, is it not pride that keeps Satan the way he is? Is it not pride that compels him to continually fight against God and His people? Let it not be once mentioned among the children of God that they believe themselves to be more than the Creator and Sustainer of the universe. How could we ever lift ourselves above the One who saved our souls? How could we possibly believe that we were capable of doing something apart from Him? How could we ever believe that we are more than God Almighty?

Fighting Against God

"But He giveth more grace. Wherefore He saith, "God resisteth the proud, but giveth grace unto the humble"" (James 4:6).

We love to review and quote the story of Job to confirm that not all human suffering is not brought on by sin. We enjoy telling others (and ourselves) that we are simply going through a test. While I do, of course, agree with the Word of God, not all hardships are brought on by sin. Some of us are actually being put to the test...but if we would be honest (which I hope you would be), sin causes death and destruction in our lives. We love to blame others for the dilemmas we find ourselves in, when in all actuality, the real cause of problems is sin (Romans 6:23). If we would be open and honest, most of us would admit our afflictions are brought on by our foolish pride.

The Greek word used for resist is 'antitasso', which is defined as "to oppose or rebel". Therefore, if you are functioning in pride, God is resisting you. He is opposed, against, and the direct enemy of the proud. There are so many areas in our lives that are in utter chaos and turmoil because of the "resistance" of the Lord. The three main areas that pride attacks are the home (Genesis 4:8), our work (Genesis 3:17-19), and our church. Continually, Satan roams from place to place seeking how he can control these areas of our lives. Consider this: Your pride may be the cause of your broken home. Pride may be the cause of your shattered career. Your foolish pride could be the cause of the relentless destruction with your church.

Don't blame someone else! Be a man/woman of integrity and confess before the Almighty God of Israel, "I have a pride issue!"

Jesus' Temptation – Israel's Wilderness

"And he brought Him to Jerusalem, and set Him on a pinnacle of the temple, and said unto Him, "If thou be the Son of God, cast thyself down from hence"" (Luke 4:9).

Living in a world of unbelievers, Jesus could be very frustrated at their refusal to accept Him. With this knowledge, Satan believed he had an opportunity to bring Christ down. Jesus was tempted to perform some spectacular feat that would prove once and for all that He was, indeed, the Son of God. For instance, He could jump from the top of the temple in front of the people, asking God to keep Him from hurt. However, to call upon God to deliver Him from an act of suicide would be a sin. It would be putting God to the test by demanding that He act in a certain way merely to satisfy an individual's selfish desire. In the end, Jesus greatly conquered that temptation as well.

We are often tempted to prove who we are. "Show me!" "Give me an example!" "Give us a demonstration!" Unless the Holy Spirit is guiding you to act, pride is knocking at your door.

"And Jesus answering said unto him, "It is said, "Thou shalt not tempt the Lord thy God"" (Luke 4:12).

"Ye shall not tempt the LORD your God, as ye tempted Him in Massah" (Deuteronomy 6:16).

To tempt (test) is to try one with either a good or evil intent. God is said to examine His people when He puts their faith and patience to the test for the sake of exercising and strengthening those graces (Hebrews 11:17). Satan and evil people are said to test others when they put their virtue to the test with the aim of seducing them into sin (Galatians 6:1). People are said to test God when they put His patience, faithfulness, or power to the test (Acts 5:9). That is a sin because our Father is always good and never changes; therefore, there is no need to put Him to the test.

It was in that way that the Israelites tested God in the desert. There would have been no sin in asking for water. In fact, our Father encourages us to come to Him with our humble requests "as little children". The Israelites severely contended with their God-given leader: Moses. The verb (contend) is often used by the prophets to describe a judicial dispute (Micah 6:2). Here, however, it means a grumpy complaining - very similar to their historical murmuring (Exodus 16:8). Moses judged this to be a challenge to God's faithful mercy and evidence of unbelief in His provision. I can imagine Moses asking the people, "Why do you distrust God? Why do you not look for comfort without habitually complaining?" That was not the first time the people had thoughtlessly rallied against Moses. Sadly, it wasn't the last (Exodus 17:1-7).

So often, the Holy Spirit has convicted me with a barrage of questions such as:

"Why are you complaining?"

"Has God ever failed you?"

"Hasn't He always provided for you?"

The command is clear: **We should not tempt the Lord.**

Everyday Jesus

"Let this mind be in you, which was also in Christ Jesus: Who, being in the form of God, thought it not robbery to be equal with God: But made Himself of no reputation, and took upon Him the form of a servant, and was made in the likeness of men" (Philippians 2:5-7).

Those verses present one of the most significant statements in all Scripture on the nature of the Incarnation (God became man). Also, through this wonderful description of Christ, Paul vividly illustrates the principle of humility. All godly actions begin with the "renewing of the mind". Right thinking produces right actions. Our actions are the fruit of our deepest thoughts, whether good or bad. Thinking and being like Christ are requirements not only for an individual, but also for the corporate body of believers. Together, we need to think and act like one being - like the person of Jesus Christ. That is why I love the Scripture that tells us, "...be we have the mind of Christ" (1 Corinthians 2:16). No matter what you have been through...no matter what obstacles you have faced...it is possible for you to think like our Savior. If your thoughts are His thoughts, your actions will be like His actions as well.

Referring to the referenced passage of Scripture, the word "servant" refers to the lowest status on the social ladder - the exact opposite of the term 'Lord'. It is truly amazing that the Lord of hosts - the One who created the universe (John 1:3) and rules over all creation (Colossians 1:17) - would choose to add to His person the nature of a servant. The phrase can be translated to mean "He emptied Himself". Emmanuel did so by taking on the form of a servant...a mere man. In doing that, He did not lose any part of His essence as God. Instead, He gave up His privileges as God and took upon Himself existence as a man. While remaining completely God, He became completely human. He that was rich became poor so that we who were poor might become rich (abundantly supplied) (2 Corinthians 8:9).

Our Passover (1 Corinthians 5:7) added to His divine essence a servant's essence - that is, the essential characteristics of a human being seeking to fulfill the will of God. Paul does not say Christ exchanged the form of a servant, involving a loss of deity or the attributes of deity. Rather, in the incarnation, Christ continued in the very nature of God, but added to Himself the very nature of a servant.

The life of Jesus speaks volumes about how to live as a servant before the Lord. God spoke of the coming Messiah as His Servant and the One who would flawlessly obey His will (Isaiah 41:1-4). Earlier in the book of Isaiah, the Lord asked, *"Whom shall I send, and who will go for us?"* We then read Isaiah's ready response: *"Here am I! Send me!"* (Isaiah 6:8). Isaiah's willingness proceeded from a grateful heart. He wanted to serve the God who had so graciously forgiven him (Isaiah 6:7). That is the prepared response of a servant's heart. *"If there is something that needs to be done – no matter how great or small – I will do it for you, Lord."*

God is not seeking the most qualified or talented; rather, He is in search of hearts that are completely surrendered to Him. He is seeking those who are available, dependable, and willing to be used. In those lives, God will show Himself strong and He will be glorified. Talents, gifts, and abilities He can give to you. The one thing you must do is choose to have a yielded heart before an Almighty Lord.

The question remains: ***Are you available?***

My Personal Walk

No sin has caused more problems for me than the sin of pride. God was not playing when He said, "Pride goes before a great fall". Amazingly, I was not always full of arrogance and haughtiness. I can vividly remember a time when things were much different. Growing up, I actually possessed a very low self-image. To this day, it still amazes me to see what I became in such a short period of time. You may wonder what I became… I became a man who thought he was something, when I was actually nothing. I became a man who thought too much of himself and too little of others. Because of the Lord's amazing grace, He was able to elevate me to a great level of prosperity in a short period of time. However, like Uzziah, my heart would soon be lifted up in pride. That pride would quickly become my own destruction.

For me, life started with extremely low confidence. Despite the love and affection received at home, my self-image was very poor. I was the kid who wore huge, thick glasses. I was overweight, shy, and was the poster-boy for "nerds" (at least that's what I thought). It is quite remarkable how our self-image determines what we are (Proverbs 23:7) and how we deal with others. If you didn't know it, young boys seek approval from young girls. I have yet to see ladies beat down doors for overweight nerds. Due to the constant rejection from the opposite sex, I painted a negative image of myself. I began to believe that no one wanted me and that I didn't deserve to be loved (in the romantic sense).

Upon salvation, the Lord began to work on my self-image. By assuring me that my self-worth was directly tied to what He said about and has done for me, the Lord helped me see that I was alright (as long as I stuck with Him). As the years rolled on – and as the Lord molded and shaped my life – I began to feel better about myself. I wasn't that bad of a guy…but soon, I began to feel too good about myself.

It was a subtle thing – almost like growing grass. One day it wasn't all that noticeable and, before I knew it, it was out of control. There is so much truth when it is said that Satan will use whatever he can to turn you from God. In the beginning, he used low self-worth to keep me from my maximum potential in Christ; later, he would use a high self-image to keep me from my maximum potential in Christ. I would have never admitted it with my lips, but my heart cried loudly with the sounds of pride. "I'm better than you!" was the shout of my heart. Because it was in my heart, it showed in my actions. I did not properly display the love of Jesus towards others. Instead, it was all about me and how I could benefit. I would (at times) even take the Word of God to justify my sinful position.

Look at it! I would tell people, ***"God said it Himself!"***

*"I died for **YOU**."*

*"**YOU** are the head and not the tail."*

*"**YOU** are more than a conqueror."*

My heart took all of those statements as personal affirmations that somehow, I was better or more privileged than others when, in fact, God is affirming all of His children - not just me.

Then one day, as He does with most leaders, God spoke to me. I must admit: It was not His usual "sweet and heavenly" voice. *"What makes you think for one minute that you are better than anyone? The same grace it took to save you is the same grace it takes to save everyone else!"* Of course, I immediately began to interrupt with overflowing apologies, not wanting to face the reality of my foolish sin. He immediately cut me off. *"Mankind is my greatest and best creation, which includes not only you, but everyone else also! I don't make junk, so please don't treat any of my creation as thus!"* What could I say? What excuse or reasoning could I give? There was none. I was completely floored. Like Job, I had said too much for my own good - and like the Israelites, the Lord took me through a series of "wilderness" experiences to humble me. The 'pruning' process was not easy; the humbling experience was not enjoyable. If God loves me (as I know He does) and if He loves you (as I know He does), the process is necessary in order for us to be shaped and molded into the image and likeness of Jesus Christ our Lord.

From that point on, any time I'm tempted to think more of myself than I should, I'm quickly reminded of this fact: I am nothing without Christ. I'm reminded that people need the Lord. That's the only lasting value a person can ever possess.

Our Solution

"Wherefore the LORD brought upon them the captains of the host of the king of Assyria, which took Manasseh among the thorns, and bound him with fetters, and carried him to Babylon. And when he was in affliction, he besought the LORD his God, and humbled himself greatly before the God of his fathers, and prayed unto Him: and he was intreated of Him, and heard his supplication, and brought him again to Jerusalem into his kingdom. Then Manasseh knew that the LORD he was God" (2 Chronicles 33:11-13).

For some time, Babylon had been a part of the Assyrian Empire, though it had broken free on occasion - especially under the leadership of Berodach-Baladan, Hezekiah's contemporary (2 Kings 20:12). Manasseh, the son of Hezekiah, seems to have set himself to the most willful and persistent restoration of every form of abomination. All the things specifically forbidden were set up in the places sacred to the name of Jehovah; and with appalling thoroughness, he undid all that his father had done. The strong hand of God was stretched out against him, and with the Assyrians as the scourge, the king was carried away in irons, broken and defeated. In distress, his stubborn will seems to have been bent, and he cried to God for help. Notice he humbled himself. He chose to be humble. No one can make you be prideful and arrogant. Being humble is a **choice** you must make. It can ***only*** be made with the help of the Holy Spirit.

Is that not a picture of our lives? Often, God has attempted to get my attention to break my haughty attitude. It was not until I had no other choices…it was not until I was afflicted greatly by the circumstances of life…it was not until I was completely broken that I chose to humble myself before God.

To be humbled is to be subdued or to bring down. A proud, arrogant, egotistical, self-sufficient Christian bristles at the thought of each submission. *"Why should I burden God with this when I can handle it myself? I'm just not going to deal with God about this."* Such thinking and behavior goes against everything for which God created us. Such thinking - prideful thinking - has everything backwards. It takes credit away from the Giver who gives graciously and awards it to the receiver who takes without thanking. That is why God sees it as an abomination (Proverbs 16:5) - a word that, throughout Proverbs, refers to God's disgust. However, God cherishes and honors a humble, contrite (repentant) spirit from someone trying to live before the Lord. I encourage you to confess sin, worry, doubt, and fear. He already knows all, but your willingness to intimately share with Him all the details speaks volumes about the resolve of your heart.

"Likewise, ye younger, submit yourselves unto the elder. Yea, all of you be subject one to another, and be clothed with humility: for God resisteth the proud, and giveth grace to the humble. Humble yourselves therefore under the mighty hand of God, that He may exalt you in due time: Casting all your care upon Him; for He careth for you" (1 Peter 5:5-7).

Pride is a very dangerous attitude and heart condition to possess. Pride is so dangerous, both the Old and New Testaments have a great deal to say about the issue. The fall of many kings and empires have taken place due to pride. Even in knowing that, pride has continued to be one of my greatest downfalls. Thinking that I'm better than someone, believing that someone is useless, and competing with man instead of pleasing God is nothing but pride. Those were all feelings, thoughts, and emotions the Lord has had to purge from my spirit.

What right do I have to feel better than someone else? The God of Heaven and Earth does not make junk. When God made man, He had two things to say: Man is fearfully and wonderfully made (Psalm 139:14) and that man is very good (Genesis 1:31). As such, I have no place to look down on anyone else. When I keep my eyes on God, He lifts me up at the right time. As long as I'm looking down on others, I cannot look up into the loving eyes of the Lord.

Closing Thought

"We usually know what we can do,
but temptation shows us who we are."
~ Thomas Kempis

My 4th Love Letter to God

(Use this section to be honest with both God and yourself. Tell God why you LOVE HIM, what you need forgiveness for, and why you are grateful.)

THE LOVE OF JESUS

"Though I speak with the tongues of men and of angels, and have not charity, I am become as sounding brass, or a tinkling cymbal. And though I have the gift of prophecy, and understand all mysteries, and all knowledge; and though I have all faith, so that I could remove mountains, and have not charity, I am nothing. And though I bestow all my goods to feed the poor, and though I give my body to be burned, and have not charity, it profiteth me nothing. Charity suffereth long, and is kind; charity envieth not; charity vaunteth not itself, is not puffed up, doth not behave itself unseemly, seeketh not her own, is not easily provoked, thinketh no evil; rejoiceth not in iniquity, but rejoiceth in the truth; beareth all things, believeth all things, hopeth all things, endureth all things. Charity never faileth: but whether there be prophecies, they shall fail; whether there be tongues, they shall cease; whether there be knowledge, it shall vanish away. For we know in part, and we prophesy in part. But when that which is perfect is come, then that which is in part shall be done away. When I was a child, I spake as a child, I understood as a child, I thought as a child: but when I became a man, I put away childish things. For now we see through a glass, darkly; but then face to face: now I know in part; but then shall I know even as also I am known. And now abideth faith, hope, charity, these three; but the greatest of these is charity" (1Corithians 13).

"The legacy you leave is the one you live."
~ The 4th Secret of the One Minute Manager

More songs have been written about love than any other topic. It has inspired some of the world's best (and worst) poetry. It has set on fire and broken countless hearts throughout human history. Romeo and Juliet were willing to defy their parents for the sake of love. People rob corner stores and banks every day out of love (for the love of money, but out of love nonetheless). Martin Luther King, Jr. promoted nonviolent protests out of love for all people. In the same breath, many things are said about love. *Love is blind. Love is a beast. Love is a splendid thing.* Yet, for the final word on the topic, we must turn to the Holy Word of God.

From the study of Scriptures, love must be very important to the Lord. Love – God's love – is a main topic found throughout the Scriptures. From Genesis to Revelations, we can see God's handiwork being displayed in love. As we have said: The very nature of God is rooted in love. In 1 Corinthians 13, the Apostle Paul (under the inspiration of the Holy Spirit) provides the world's most beautiful ode to love. With regard to the word 'love', the Greek word "agape" occurs about 116 times in the New Testament. It is that love that's the love of Jesus. It is that love that took Him to the cross. It is the great love of Jesus that we must possess and **fully** operate in. When I truly embraced the love displayed on the cross at Calvary, it was then that I began to let go of self and cling to Jesus Christ my Lord.

"As the Father hath loved me, so have I loved you: continue ye in my love. If ye keep my commandments, ye shall abide in my love; even as I have kept my Father's commandments, and abide in his love. This is my commandment, That ye love one another, as I have loved you. Greater love hath no man than this, that a man lay down his life for his friends. Ye are my friends, if ye do whatsoever I command you. These things I command you, that ye love one another" (John 15:9 – 10, 12 – 14, 17).

There is an awesome revelation within those passages of scripture. Jesus tells us that He is only imitating the love the Father has shown Him. That is His commandment to us: that we love one another just as He has loved us. Then Jesus capped it off with a **true** spiritual challenge: *"If you really want to express the highest form of love, lay down your life for your friend."* That is not limited to stopping a bullet or chasing a mugger. **Anytime** you're willing to give of yourself (time, talent, treasure) to benefit others, you are laying down your life for a friend.

If people are true disciples, they will prove it by the fruits that their spiritual union with Jesus produces. The Fruit of the Spirit is: love, joy, peace, patience, kindness, goodness, faithfulness, gentleness, and self-control. All of those manifestations are wonderful, but the fruit we are studying here is the fruit of love. Our Father is love; therefore, His children are love (at least they should be) – but as we have previously discussed, not just any love will do. We must possess and demonstrate the love of Jesus.

Jesus' Love Toward Us

"But God commendeth His love toward us, in that, while we were yet sinners, Christ died for us" (Romans 5:8).

In Romans 5:8, Paul explains the nature of God's love. He goes into detail about what His eternal love actually looks like. God loved us when we were still without strength and ungodly. God loved us while we were lovers of darkness. God loved us while we were actually His enemies. God loved us so much, He sent His Son to die for us. The One who had done no wrong, had committed no sin, and was always in perfect fellowship…He was the one receiving the punishment on our behalf. That is what God's love looks like.

God loves us just the way we are, but He loves us too much to leave us the way we are. Therefore, He who has begun a good work in us is working and shall bring it to completion (Philippians 1:6). God's Word brings great joy to my heart. To know - not guess - but know that God loves me! Regardless of life's circumstances…regardless of who comes and goes…God loves me. Despite my shortcomings and faults, God loves me. Please don't think for one moment accidents and incidents "just happen" in our lives. All things are the powerful hand of God orchestrating the circumstances of our existence, for the Father's desire is that no man should perish, but that all should come to the knowledge of His great love (2 Peter 3:9).

We Must Follow His Example

"Be ye therefore followers of God, as dear children" (Ephesians 5:1).

Believers are to follow the example of God's actions. I am often stunned to watch my children attempt to do the things they see me do. Though they may fail hundreds of times, they keep trying until they succeed. I believe their main motivation - the reason they relentlessly continue with unyielding determination - is they want to be like their father. Just as children imitate and mimic their parents, so are we to copy our Heavenly Father. He loved us when we were still His enemies; He loved us while we were yet undeserving of His love. As imitators, believers should demonstrate that type of self-sacrificial, beneficial, and unconditional love.

How many of us are willing to bless them that curse and spitefully misuse us? How many of us are willing to bless and curse not? How many of us are ready to overcome evil with good (Romans 12:14,21)? Especially during the Christmas season, we are a "do for me and I'll do for you" people. The Christmas holiday is no longer about the birth of our Savior. It is no longer about the great redemption plan of God. Now, it's all about what I can get instead of what I can give. The love of Jesus is not like that, for there is no way we could ever repay Him for what He has done for us.

Freely we have received; freely we should give (Matthew 10:8).

Our Love Toward Others

"A new commandment I give unto you, That ye love one another; as I have loved you, that ye also love one another. By this shall all men know that ye are my disciples, if ye have love one to another (John 13:34 – 35)."

That command to love was new because Jesus gave it a new standard. In the Old Testament, Moses said, "Love your neighbor as yourself" (Leviticus 19:18). Jesus said the new standard was "...as I have loved you". Jesus gave His disciples the example of love that they were to follow. The same way Jesus has loved and cared for you...the same way He has looked after and cherished you...you are to love others. Whatever we do to others is what we offer to God (Matthew 25:40). Jesus said it like this: *"I was hungry and you fed me; I was thirsty and you gave me drink; I was a stranger and you took me in. I was naked and you clothed me. I was sick and you came to visit me. I was in prison and you came to me"* (Matthew 25:35-36). By that, unbelievers recognize Jesus' disciples - not by their doctrinal characteristics, nor by dramatic miracles, nor even by their lavish lifestyles. Others will recognize His disciples by their deeds of love towards all mankind.

That is the love of Jesus.

Giving is Essential in True Love

"For God so loved the world, that He gave His only begotten Son, that whosoever believeth in Him should not perish, but have everlasting life" (John 3:16).

"My little children, let us not love in word, neither in tongue; but in deed and in truth" (1 John 3:18).

We cannot honestly profess to be loving children of God if we are not a giving people. God is not a stingy God - nor are His people stingy. Love does not gather all it can for itself. Instead, love sees a need and finds a way to give. Love is more than a word or a feeling; it is an action that is to be expressed through our lives daily. If a man was to tell a woman that he loves her but never shows that love, what type of love does that man truly possess? In fact, that would not be love at all; it would merely be "lip service". That is exactly what we offer the Lord and those around us when our love is not supported by actions.

The New Testament concept of love closely parallels that of the Old Testament's concept of love. Moses writes, *"The Lord is compassionate and gracious, slow to anger, full of love and faithfulness"* (Exodus 34:6). John writes, *"Dear children, let us not love with words or tongue, but with actions and in truth"* (1 John 3:18). Believers need to share with those in need - whether that need is food, water, lodging, clothing, healing, or friendship (Matthew 25:34-40). The love demonstrated in the parable of the Good Samaritan shows that agape love is not emotional love, but a response to someone who is genuinely in need.

Is that not the very essence of who God is? God loved us so much that He selflessly did something about our immoral situation. God's love brought Himself from Heaven to Earth; Jesus' love took Him from the Earth to the cross; and His love transitioned Him from the grave back to Heaven. When we truly love as God loves, we will be people of action – not only people of words.

Finally, Love One Another

"Charity suffereth long, and is kind; charity envieth not; charity vaunteth not itself, is not puffed up, doth not behave itself unseemly, seeketh not her own, is not easily provoked, thinketh no evil; rejoiceth not in iniquity, but rejoiceth in the truth; beareth all things, believeth all things, hopeth all things, endureth all things. Charity never faileth: but whether there be prophecies, they shall fail; whether there be tongues, they shall cease; whether there be knowledge, it shall vanish away" (1 Corinthians 13:4 – 8).

'Charity' in those verses is translated in the English language as love, but not just any type of love. There are at least four Greek words for love, not all of which are in the New Testament: *Agape, Philos, Philstonges,* and *Eros*. Therefore, God's love can be a very broad topic. It can also be very short and simple. If you desire to only be shallow and surface-level, the Lord can be that. If you desire to take your relationship with Him to new and deeper depths, He is able and more than willing to accomplish that in your life.

The Lord's written Word gives us great insight to instruct us in love along life's journey. 1 Corinthians 13 gives us some specifics regarding what the love of Jesus is…and is not. Hence, we take a look at the Scriptures so we will know when our thoughts and actions are flowing from He whom my soul eternally loves (Song of Solomon 3:4).

- **Longsuffering (patient)** – suffers long; to have patience, to exhibit internal and external control in difficult circumstances. The love of Jesus patiently bears frustrations and is not quick to stress its rights and is not quick to be offended by an injury.

"And they that passed by reviled Him, wagging their heads, and saying, "Thou that destroyest the temple, and buildest it in three days, save thyself. If thou be the Son of God, come down from the cross." Likewise also the chief priests mocking him, with the scribes and elders, said, "He saved others; Himself he cannot save. If He be the King of Israel, let Him now come down from the cross, and we will believe Him. He trusted in God; let Him deliver Him now, if He will have Him: for He said, I am the Son of God"" (Matthew 27:39 – 43).

Jesus would not come down from the cross just because He was the Son of God and the King of Israel (John 10:18). That would have been defiant disobedience on His part. However, on the contrary, He obediently followed God's plan for Him. His obedience would ultimately lead to His exaltation as King over all (Philippians 2:8-11). That is a title no one has ever or will ever be able to claim. If Jesus needed to exercise patience, how much more do we need to practice His patience in our lives? How much more do we need the Holy Spirit (working within us) to assist us in exercising internal and external control?

It was Jesus' love for us that allowed Him to stay on the cross. It was His love for mankind that allowed Him to patiently endure. It was His love for the sinful fallen human race that allowed Him to exhibit great internal and external control in a very difficult position.

- **Love is kind** - The root of the Greek verb means "useful". Those who express the love of Jesus will convey pleasant deeds to help - not deeds of hurt.

"How God anointed Jesus of Nazareth with the Holy Ghost and with power: who went about doing good, and healing all that were oppressed of the devil; for God was with Him" (Acts 10:38).

Long before the cross, Jesus was walking the Earth performing good deeds for mankind. Healing the sick, raising the dead, feeding the poor, and clothing the naked…that is love in action. Through the grace of Jesus Christ, let us find ourselves being useful and helpful to our fellow man.

Oftentimes, we are looking to some large and grand performance of love, when many times, it is the small, unsuspecting gestures that mean the most - a genuine hug, a friendly smile, giving someone a ride…those and many more are kind acts of love.

- **Love does not envy** - a negative attitude of lust and desire for another's possessions.

"And John answered him, saying, "Master, we saw one casting out devils in thy name, and he followeth not us: and we forbad him, because he followeth not us." But Jesus said, "Forbid him not: for there is no man which shall do a miracle in My name, that can lightly speak evil of Me. For he that is not against us is on our part"" (Mark 9:38 – 40).

God's Word was to spread to everyone who was willing to accept the truth of who He is. God's work was not necessarily restricted to their small twelve-man group (the disciples). Jesus was not worried or jealous because of that man's actions. In fact, it brought Him great joy! Jesus was not attempting to put the spotlight solely on Himself. If we look at His ministry, Jesus always deferred the attention off of Himself and appropriately placed it on God the Father. Jesus' love does not express wrong feelings from the good others receive. That includes hatred, rivalry, and so on. Envy inevitably leads to personal harm and debilitation, while affecting one's physical, spiritual, and emotional well-being (Proverbs 14:30). Unchecked, it gradually leads to a destructive and remorseful way of life (Proverbs 27:4) and, ultimately, to estrangement from God (Romans 1:28-32).

- **Not puffed up** - to be proud or arrogant. Is not proud (that is the root of boasting). Love, on the other hand, is modest and humble. Anyone who has a high opinion of himself is apt to be boastful and desire praise. God opposes the proud (Proverbs 3:34). That caused Satan's fall as well.

"Then answered Jesus and said unto them, "Verily, verily, I say unto you, The Son can do nothing of Himself, but what He seeth the Father do: for what things soever He doeth, these also doeth the Son likewise"" (John 5:19).

Pride is the direct opposite of humility. Pride says, *"I am self-sufficient";* humility says, *"I can do nothing without the Lord's help"*. Pride goes before a great fall; humility goes before great exaltation. Jesus - God in the flesh - recognized His limitations while on Earth. Just like any man, he would hunger, thirst, sleep, and would even feel pain. Jesus openly acknowledged that apart from God the Father, He could do nothing. That is our guide to walking this life in total victory. That is a humble servant's heart.

- **Love does not behave rudely** - to act improperly, dishonorably, indecently, or rudely. Love's whole behavior is respectable and attractive.

"Think not that I am come to destroy the law, or the prophets; I am not come to destroy, but to fulfil" (Matthew 5:17).

Jesus wanted all to know that He understood the "way of doing things" in their Jewish culture. Christ knew very well that the laws were given of God; therefore, the law was a good thing and was not to be thrown aside. Christ was there to fulfill the law in every area and in every way (keep the law where we were disobedient). He was able to bring a revolution to the hearts and minds of all mankind, while at the same time behaving with honor, decency, dignity, and respect.

- **Not her own will** – is not self-seeking.

"And He went a little further, and fell on His face, and prayed, saying, "O my Father, if it be possible, let this cup pass from me: nevertheless, not as I will, but as Thou wilt"" (Matthew 26:39).

It was not the impending physical suffering – as terrible as it would be – that caused Jesus to pray that way. It was the reality of the sinless Son of God bearing the sins of the world and facing separation from His Father (Hebrews 12:2). That is difficult for us to understand, but Jesus (who had never been separated from the Father) could not bear the mere thought of the strain on their relationship. That verse also shows Jesus' active submission to the Father's will (as is recorded in Matthew 26:42). Jesus did not go reluctantly, but with determination to do the Father's blessed will. Even though Jesus had full knowledge of the suffering that was to come, He was obedient to the will of our Most High God.

Can we be so bold to say the same? Regardless of the sorrow or suffering – not our will, but Thine will be done!

- **Rejoices in the truth** - corresponding to reality.

"Sanctify them through thy truth; thy word is truth" (John 17:17).

Christians should not drift through life making decisions according to what looks or feels best. Wise men and women - those who seek the truth to guide them through life - can avoid the snare of poor choices and negative consequences. We all know the only perfectly dependable source of truth is God's Holy Word. Living by biblical principles protects believers from the enemy's deceptions. If we look at Jesus (our perfect example), He never contradicts Scripture - for He is the very Word of God in the flesh! His earthly life was always guided by God's Holy Word. In the same way, we (as "little Christs") should live according to God's Holy Word.

- **Bears all things** – to put up with, stand, to protect, cover. Love is loyal, no matter the cost. Love always protects.

"The next day, John seeth Jesus coming unto him, and saith, "Behold the Lamb of God, which taketh away the sin of the world"" (John 1:29).

In order for Jesus to hold true to that title, He had to bear the heavy sins of the world upon Himself. That was no easy task; it was the greatest task ever undertaken. What a great load He willingly took to only bear my sins, for great was the sinfulness of my dreadfully unredeemed soul. When I think of the accumulated sins of all people (past, present, and future), "bearing all things" is the greatest height of love. Even now, He sits at the right hand of the Father, affectionately interceding for us, and continuing to bear our problems and concerns before the throne of God.

- **Believes all things** - put one's faith in, with an implication that actions based on that trust will follow. Love expects the best from people.

"Afterward Jesus findeth him in the temple, and said unto him, "Behold, thou art made whole: sin no more, lest a worse thing come unto thee"" (John 5:14).

Jesus had just healed a man of his disease. Later, Jesus locates him in the temple. One thing He tells the man that is truly amazing is: "Sin no more." We must realize and understand that our Lord does not waste words. He does not talk just for the fun of it. Therefore, if our Blessed Hope tells you to sin no more, that's exactly what He expects. Furthermore, He must believe that you are capable of living a holy life; otherwise, He would not have told you to do so.

Let us look and treat others in like-fashion, hoping and believing the best for their lives - not being naïve, but believing and hoping for the best that God has for their lives.

- **Hopes all things** - an attitude of confidently looking forward to what is good and beneficial. Love always hopes (hopes for the best with regard to everyone).

"And the Lord said, "Simon, Simon, behold, Satan hath desired to have you, that he may sift you as wheat: but I have prayed for thee, that thy faith fail not: and when thou art converted, strengthen thy brethren"" (Luke 22:31 – 32).

The Greek word for 'you' in verse 31 is plural, indicating that Satan had asked permission to trouble all the disciples. In verse 32, the Greek word for 'you' is singular, referring specifically to Peter.

In effect, Jesus restored Peter even before his fall, and He instructed the disciples to shepherd the saints by strengthening them. Remarkably, God treats us as we someday shall be - not as we currently appear. Throughout the Scriptures, He calls us sons and daughters, kings and priests, and the righteous and redeemed. Although we may not always feel like it, God has a great hope and promise for what we shall someday become.

May God's Spirit bless us with the ability to treat others as they shall someday become in the mighty hands of God. Amen.

- **Love never fails** - to be dashed to pieces, taken none effect. Love wins in every situation. No matter the circumstances, love is the answer.

"For God so loved the world, that He gave His only begotten Son; that whosoever believeth in Him should not perish, but have everlasting life" (John 3:16).

Love - God's love - is the answer for every problem…in every situation…for all times. As a child, I remember singing the song "Jesus is the answer for all the world today… Above Him, there's no other; Jesus is the way". Whether it be family, job, school, government, or church-related, His love is the solution to the varied messes we find ourselves in. Jesus solved mankind's greatest dilemma once and for all with His great love. It is His great love that continues to draw us - even today (Hosea 11:4). If you are ever in doubt as to how or what you should do, look at the love of Jesus. His love is our ever-shining example and guide.

Closing Thought

"Love is the true price of love."
~ George Hebert

My 5th Love Letter to God

(Use this section to be honest with both God and yourself. Tell God why you LOVE HIM, what you need forgiveness for, and why you are grateful.)

DO YOU LOVE ME?

"Jesus saith unto them, "Come and dine." And none of the disciples durst ask Him, "Who art thou?" knowing that it was the Lord. Jesus then cometh, and taketh bread, and giveth them, and fish likewise. This is now the third time that Jesus shewed himself to His disciples, after that He was risen from the dead. So when they had dined, Jesus saith to Simon Peter, "Simon, son of Jonas, lovest thou me more than these?" He saith unto him, "Yea, Lord; thou knowest that I love thee." He saith unto him, "Feed my lambs." He saith to him again the second time, "Simon, son of Jonas, lovest thou me?" He saith unto him, "Yea, Lord; thou knowest that I love thee." He saith unto him, "Feed my sheep." He saith unto him the third time, "Simon, son of Jonas, lovest thou me?" Peter was grieved because he said unto him the third time, "Lovest thou me?" And he said unto Him, "Lord, thou knowest all things; thou knowest that I love thee." Jesus saith unto him, "Feed my sheep. Verily, verily, I say unto thee, When thou wast young, thou girdedst thyself, and walkedst whither thou wouldest: but when thou shalt be old, thou shalt stretch forth thy hands, and another shall gird thee, and carry thee whither thou wouldest not." This spake He, signifying by what death He should glorify God. And when He had spoken this, He saith unto him, "Follow me"" (John 21:12 – 19).

"Without a change in behavior, just saying "I'm sorry" is not enough."
~ The 4th Secret of the One Minute Manager

YES
NO
MAYBE

The Spirit of the Lord came to me in great power in November 2006 during a Women's Day worship service. The Almighty led me to and through the previous parts of this book three months prior. He allowed me time to "sink my teeth" into the lust of the flesh, the lust of the eyes, and the pride of life. He gave me time to understand just where my sin originated. He allowed me to see just how detrimental I was to myself. Now, standing in the doorway of a new revelation, like His disciples, I, too, had to admit: "This is a hard saying." A lot of time had passed and I was seemingly no better than when I first began the voyage.

I was well aware of my plight, but my real challenge was determining how to fix my situation. How do I overcome the obstacles that so easily turn me aside? How do I 'die to self' daily? How do I pick up my cross and follow Christ? That is what was required of me, therefore, I pressed on. Though feeling undone, unworthy, and so unfaithful, to top it off, I now felt overwhelmed. Though overwhelmed, the Lord would add one more ingredient to the mix. On that evening, through His Word, Jesus asked me a question that still chills me to this day: *"Do you love Me?"* I am utterly amazed at how God drives us to the end of ourselves so we can realize He's all we really need.

Sitting there during that worship service, I was not concerned with my physical appearance; I was not concerned with the people around me, for I was in the presence of the Great Jehovah. All I could focus on was the will of God for my life. I knew the command to love God. I knew I should love God; I knew I wanted to love God…but how? How does someone so undone love Someone so complete? I had no valid answer for His question; therefore, He asked twice more: *"Do you love Me?"* or (in English terms) *"What type of love do you have for Me?"*

With His words still ringing in my ears and penetrating through to my heart, living streams of water began to spring forth from my eyes. I began to shake my head in disbelief, not wanting to face the truth that stood before me. In my heart, I covered my face in shame and regret. Could it be true? Was my heart not completely yielded to the Lord? Could it be that I did not truly love our Blessed Hope (1 Timothy 1:1) with all my heart? As Simon said (and I, too, had to admit), "Lord, you know all things. You know what type of love I have for you." It grieves me greatly to know that I've loved my Savior with anything less than what He deserves. Through great sorrow and distress, through great tears and heartache, the Lord revealed a great truth to me.

Without the Lord, we are totally incapable of loving God or others (a condition that must be corrected by God). The Bible's ways of describing this process of correction are numerous, to include: *"circumcision of the heart"* (Deuteronomy 30:6); *God's substituting of a "heart of flesh" for a "heart of stone"* (Ezekiel 11:19); and *"moving out of darkness into light"* (1 John 2:9). Until that happens - until Jesus Christ becomes active within us - we cannot properly convey God's love. That is what Jesus is asking us: ***"Do you love Me with God's love?"*** Sure, most of us hold Jesus in a high regard, but have we placed Him above all…even before ourselves? Even demons reverence the name of Jesus. Have you submitted everything (thoughts, actions, and decisions) to the reign of Jesus Christ?

If only taken at face value, a great treasure will be missed while reading the Scriptures shared within the pages of this book. The love that Jesus spoke of was very different from the love Simon spoke of. Jesus spoke of "agape" love. Agape love is a selfless love; the type of love which characterizes God. That is a love that only the Lord of Hosts is able to show, yet it is that type of love He commands us to show.

John affirms that by saying, "God is love" (1 John 4:8). God does not merely love; He is love! Everything God does flows from His love. Agape love is an act of the will rather than of the emotions. God loves us because He chooses to love us, not because we deserve it or have somehow merited His love. He loves us simply because He has chosen to do so. Is that not a wonderful blessing?

Despite my sins…even with all my guilt and shame…no matter how many times I reject Christ………He still loves me! He loves me with an endless, immeasurable, favorable, bountiful love. Oh, how that revelation warms the very depths of my soul to know and understand that our Heavenly Father ***"agape"*** loves me!

On the other hand, Simon spoke of "phileo" love. Phileo love is affection and regard of a very high order, but it is not an eternal, everlasting, sacrificial, beneficial, and unconditional love. Phileo love is a strong fondness; to treat affectionately or kindly; to strongly like. The love Simon spoke of was nothing more than the fondness found in a casual friendship. God desires to be more than just a laid-back friend. He wants to be the Lover of your soul and the One whom your soul loves. He wishes to be everything for you. Above all, He wishes to have a loving and personal relationship with you.

Simon Peter had once boasted that he loved the Son of God more than the other disciples did, and that although ***they*** might fail Him, he would not (Mark 14:29) - yet three times, he publicly disowned Jesus. Three times, Peter stated he did not have a relationship with Jesus Christ. Three times, he was asked publicly if he loved Jesus as a reminder to him of the danger of overconfidence. Jesus' public conversation with Peter also showed the others that He had forgiven him. As a leader in that early group, Peter would need more love for Jesus than the others. If Peter was to follow Jesus, he would no longer be free to live the independent life of an energetic, young fisherman. His life would be one of constant sacrifice and hard work in caring for Jesus' people. In the end, he would be captured and killed on account of his love for Jesus.

Jesus still asks the same question even today: *"Do you love Me?"*

When my mind reflects on all that Jesus' precious blood has done for me, it is His blood that has cleansed me, healed me, helped me to overcome, and given me access to the Father.

When I ponder just what His grace and mercy have done in my life, it is God's grace that turns His wrath that I so rightfully deserve. It is His grace that opens to me all spiritual blessings in heavenly places.

When I think of those things and more, an agonizing pain shoots through my heart because I realize: 'I don't love the Lord as I should'. A shame comes over me when I think: 'I'm incapable of loving the Lord as I should'.

When I think of the goodness of Jesus and all He has done for me…when I think of my wretchedness and all the times I've denied Christ…oh, the regret that fills my heart.

Even still, there is something amazing about failure. Times of failure not only reveal a person's true character, but also present opportunities for significant life lessons. Like Peter, I have cried tears of sorrow and shame. Like Paul, I've asked, "Who shall deliver me from this flesh?" Like David, I come to the Lord admitting that I have sinned and desperately need forgiveness.

In the Beginning – A Test of Love

"Now the serpent was more subtil than any beast of the field which the LORD God had made. And he said unto the woman, "Yea, hath God said, "Ye shall not eat of every tree of the garden?"" And the woman said unto the serpent, "We may eat of the fruit of the trees of the garden: But of the fruit of the tree which is in the midst of the garden, God hath said, Ye shall not eat of it, neither shall ye touch it, lest ye die." And the serpent said unto the woman, "Ye shall not surely die: For God doth know that in the day ye eat thereof, then your eyes shall be opened, and ye shall be as gods, knowing good and evil." And when the woman saw that the tree was good for food, and that it was pleasant to the eyes, and a tree to be desired to make one wise, she took of the fruit thereof, and did eat, and gave also unto her husband with her; and he did eat" (Genesis 3:1–6).

Of all who have ever lived, Eve was the only one who could legitimately use the phrase, "The devil made me do it". God did not accept that excuse from Eve - and she had the serpent speaking directly to her! If He did not accept it from her, surely He will not accept it from us. We cannot pass the buck for sinning to anyone else. God wants us to understand the true source of sin so that we can come to terms with it honestly before Him. Satan has always tested our love for the Father. In every situation and decision, our love for God the Father, God the Son, and God the Holy Spirit is being tried by fire to see what sort of love it is.

Jesus said it this way: *"If you love me, you'll keep my commandments"* (John 14:15); *"Why call me your Lord and do not as I say?"* (Luke 6:46); and *"If you do as I say, you'll abide in my love; just as I've kept my Father's commandments, and abide in His love"* (John 15:10).

The first Adam failed to completely and perfectly express his love for the Creator, for Adam failed to be obedient. Just like skin color, personality, and hair, that same sin character trait has been passed on to us. We fail to properly express our love to God because we fail to remain obedient to His commands.

There will always be temptation vying for our hearts, but we must decide who or what we love the most. When it comes to God and the things of this world, there is only one choice. As Simon Peter said, "Where else can we go? You have the words of eternal life" (John 6:68). Those who find themselves at the Savior's feet choose humble devotion over worldly prestige, power, and fame. Oftentimes, we make our relationship with God complicated; but love is never complex when it comes to God. He loves us without hesitation, and that is what He longs for from us in return. He longs that we love Him with our whole mind, with our whole body, and with our whole soul.

Without hesitation…without reservation…without vacillation, our hearts should cry out to our loving Creator in obedient surrender and affection.

Jesus' Temptation – A Test of Love

"And Jesus being full of the Holy Ghost returned from Jordan, and was led by the Spirit into the wilderness, being forty days tempted of the devil. And in those days He did eat nothing: and when they were ended, He afterward hungered. And the devil said unto him, "If thou be the Son of God, command this stone that it be made bread." And Jesus answered him, saying, "It is written, that man shall not live by bread alone, but by every word of God." And the devil, taking Him up into an high mountain, shewed unto Him all the kingdoms of the world in a moment of time. And the devil said unto him, "All this power will I give thee, and the glory of them: for that is delivered unto me; and to whomsoever I will I give it. If thou therefore wilt worship me, all shall be thine." And Jesus answered and said unto him, "Get thee behind me, Satan: for it is written, thou shalt worship the Lord thy God, and Him only shalt thou serve." And he brought Him to Jerusalem, and set Him on a pinnacle of the temple, and said unto Him, "If thou be the Son of God, cast thyself down from hence: For it is written, He shall give His angels charge over thee, to keep thee: And in their hands they shall bear thee up, lest at any time thou dash thy foot against a stone." And Jesus answering said unto him, "It is said, thou shalt not tempt the Lord thy God." And when the devil had ended all the temptation, he departed from Him for a season" (Luke 4:1 – 13).

Everyone faces temptation. Even the Son of God was tempted by Satan to walk away from God. Jesus saw through the enemy's schemes and remained firm in His love and devotion to the Father (Luke 4:1-13). As with Jesus, we don't struggle with our emotions or our bodies. The real enemy isn't even Satan. For every problem and every concern we may have, we struggle with a decision.

That is why Joshua told the people to choose whom they would serve (Joshua 24:15). The Scripture states that God has presented us with life and death. He admonishes us to choose life. It is in choosing life or death that we express love or hate, faith or unbelief, and peace or turmoil towards the Father. If Satan could get Jesus to not perfectly love God, he could get Him to disobey. However, Jesus always pleased the Father, for He always obeyed the Father. Regardless of how it felt and no matter what the skeptics had to say, even in the face of Satan, Christ always chose to obey.

I know that many will have a problem with me stating Satan is not our real enemy. Look at it from this perspective: So often, we give Satan too much credit. Satan is fallen. He cannot foretell the future. He is limited in space and time; he can only be in one place at a time. He is not eternal. It is impossible for Satan to make you sin. Sin is a choice. Satan can tempt us, but we decide to sin. *"By his own evil desire, he is dragged away and enticed"* (James 1:14). Since the devil is unable to **make** us sin, we need to reconsider blaming him for our wrong choices. The bigger enemy is the lust of our flesh, the lust of our eyes, and the pride within us. To square off against Satan is easy by comparison. Those things must be subdued daily - even momentarily. That's why the Scriptures say, "For the...Spirit desires what is contrary to the sinful nature". The battle is already won against Satan. The ongoing battle is with our sinful fallen nature.

Temptation: The Two Adams Contrasted

Both Adam and Christ faced three aspects of temptation. Adam yielded, bringing upon humankind sin and death. Christ resisted, resulting in justification and life.		
1 John 2:16	**Genesis 3:6 First Adam**	**Luke 4:1–13 Second Adam – Christ**
"The Lust of the Flesh"	"the tree was good for food"	"command this stone to become bread"
"The Lust of the Eyes"	"it was pleasant to the eyes"	"the devil…showed Him all the kingdoms"
"The Pride of Life"	"a tree desirable to make one wise"	"throw Yourself down from here"

Jesus' Victory

"Saying, "Father, if thou be willing, remove this cup from me: nevertheless, not my will, but thine be done"" (Luke 22:42).

The Holy One of God (Mark 1:24) agonized over His approaching death and the effects of God's wrath. The mere thought of being separated from the Father caused Jesus great pain. Even in the midst of His great mission, Jesus was still only concerned about what His Father wanted. Jesus said, "The Son can do nothing of Himself" (John 5:30). In other places, He says He can do nothing independent of the Father.

Have you ever agonized over a choice you had to make? Can we be so bold and say we will do the same? That theme can be traced from the very beginning of time. It was Jesus who gave up immortality and put on a body that was prepared for Him (Hebrews 10:5). He wasn't concerned with His own affliction. He suffered the humiliation of the cross to redeem fallen mankind.

Everyday Jesus

"As the Father hath loved me, so have I loved you: continue ye in my love. If ye keep my commandments, ye shall abide in my love; even as I have kept my Father's commandments, and abide in His love" (John 15:9 – 10).

John declares: *"This is how we know what love is: Jesus Christ laid down His life for us"* (1 John 3:16). What exactly does that mean? It means He was obedient even till death. Even though it would cost Jesus His life, He was determined to love the Father and be completely submissive. That is God's love. God's love is not based on the merit of the recipient (Romans 5:7-8). His love for us cannot be earned or bought or even won. His love for us just "is", because He is love. Because He is love, God is not willing that any person should perish, but wills that everyone repent and live (Ezekiel 18:32).

God is unlike the gods of the heathen. They hate and are angry. God is unlike the gods of the philosopher. They are cold and indifferent. Our God loves us with a personal and cherished love. He is concerned with every large and small aspect of our lives. Whether you realize it or not, the Lord is working to reveal His great love to you in a very unique way. I suppose we could call God the ***"Ultimate Macro and Micro Manager"***!

My Personal Walk

At the end of the day, after all is said and done, my love for the Lord is directly tied to my obedience to Him. Through my obedience, I not only express love; I also show Him great honor and respect. It has been tough to wrap my mind around this concept, for it is, indeed, a hard saying. I would like to believe that my love for God remains the same - regardless of my thoughts and actions. Sadly, I know this is far from the truth. Because of how sinful I am…because of how fallen mankind is…because of the darkening effects of sin…my will still fights with God (a losing battle if ever there was one). I've come to realize that is the true battle.

I have not been fighting sexual desires.

I wasn't struggling with laziness.

Overeating was not the real problem.

On the hill of all of life's choices, every day - in every way - I was struggling with submitting my will to God's will. If I could submit to God's will in every situation, there would be no battle; there would be no internal resistance. The continual answer of my heart and soul would be, *"Yes, Lord! Yes, to Your will and yes to Your way!"*

Since the struggle is an everyday occurrence, my life is filled with moments of my carnal will versus the Lord's holy will. I would like to select a significant event in my life to fully-illustrate this principle. Can I really choose just one moment, though? All of life's decisions now seem so important under the light of that wonderful revelation. The times God warned me of an illicit relationship, but I chose to uncaringly pursue it anyway…that was a choice of my will. When I elected to demean and humiliate others with upsetting words…my will was not given over to Jesus. Even in those moments when I fixed my mind on things unholy instead of being led by the Spirit, I chose to do as I pleased.

On the other hand, when I was determined to pray for my enemies (as badly as I desired to do them harm), I surrendered to God's will. The surrender completely eliminated the struggle. When I was tempted to listen to secular music that God was slowly weaning me from and chose, instead, to worship Him in song, I yielded to the magnificent lordship of Jesus. Often, thoughts of superiority would quickly rise in my spirit, thinking to myself: *"Why do I have to suffer? Why must I have such a difficult life?"* When I realigned my thoughts with the mind of Christ, victory was mine!

Ultimately, we win when we lose. That's a difficult concept for a competitive person such as myself to comprehend. ***"You lose when you win? What world is that and how do I get there?"*** When I lose to the Holy Spirit and He has full control, that's when I succeed. I grew up thinking I had to work harder or pray more, sometimes feeling like if I just loved God more or served Him better, I thought I could conquer my flesh, my eyes, and my pride. All of those things are good…but alone, they mean nothing. Countless times, God has reminded me: "Above everything you can do for me, obedience is the thing I want the most." All along, it was so simple; I just needed to give in to God. Just as easily as I chose to give in to Satan and his pull, I could elect to give in to God! I now understand why Paul tells us to die to self. I now understand why Jesus tells us to deny ourselves daily.

I must die.

I must surrender.

I must lose in the battle.

When I "wave the flag of surrender" and allow the Holy Spirit to triumph, I WIN! It feels good to be able to finally say it:

"When I surrender, I WIN!"

Our Solution

"Beloved, let us love one another: for love is of God; and every one that loveth is born of God, and knoweth God. He that loveth not knoweth not God; for God is love. Whosoever shall confess that Jesus is the Son of God, God dwelleth in him, and he in God. And we have known and believed the love that God hath to us. God is love; and he that dwelleth in love dwelleth in God, and God in him" (1 John 4:7-8, 15–16).

There are five key areas that will assist us in our journey to properly loving God:

1. **Salvation** - *The justification (declared innocent or righteous), the sanctification (the initial and continual removal of sin), and the glorification (the final removal of sin where one becomes like Christ) of a person from sin. This is only accomplished through the acceptance of the death, burial, and resurrection of Jesus Christ (the Son of God) as atonement for your sins (Romans 10:1 – 4).*

The first step in knowing the Lord is found in what the Firstborn (Colossians 1:15) has done for us. If we cannot accept what His Son has done for us, we cannot and will not love the Lord and others. If you should die today, where would you spend eternity? No one likes to think about dying, but death comes to everyone. 10 out of 10 people die. That includes you! That is a mind-blowing and heart-chilling statistic! Since you must die, you must prepare to meet God. When you were born into this world, you inherited a sinful nature. That corrupt character produces all sorts of evil deeds. God declares that the result of sin is eternal physical and spiritual death.

There is nothing you can do to save yourself from that saddening plight. You cannot be "good enough"; neither can you be saved by keeping the law. Joining the church and being baptized will not help save you. Following are the things that must be done in order for you to be saved from your sin.

a) Admit that you are a sinner in need of a Savior (Romans 3:23).
b) Believe what Jesus has done for you (Romans 5:8).
c) Confess with your mouth what you believe (Romans 10:13).

"Nay, in all these things, we are more than conquerors through Him that loved us" (Romans 8:37).

So many times, I have felt as if my various situations and circumstances in life were hopeless. I have tried to stop, but I just can't seem to do it. I have prayed. I have cried. I have fasted. I have even asked the church to pray for me – to no avail. I couldn't seem to let go; I couldn't stop. I have read and known Romans 8:37 for quite some time, but I have never known it like I do now. I usually place the focus on other parts of the Scripture. Yes: I AM a conqueror! Yes: I can do all things through Christ who strengthens me! Yes: I am the head and not the tail! But why? Why am I such a great conqueror? Is it because of the family I was born into? Is it because I'm so lucky? Maybe it's because I work and try so hard… Am I such a wonderful conqueror because I'm just good at what I do? The answer to each and every question is "no". None of those aspects truly matter, for none of them will assist you or me in overcoming our sin nature.

Countless individuals have tried and failed on their own. I have always believed that if a person could accomplish those things on their own, they would already be done. Because we have yet to overcome certain areas, we must be waiting for and be in need of help. That help comes from the Holy Spirit. There is no one who has honestly tried to prevail with God's help and failed, for in Christ, we are always triumphant!

The reason we can proclaim to be a conqueror is because of the awesome love of Jesus Christ our Lord. It is His love that brought Him from Heaven to Earth. It is His immense love that carried Him all the way to the cross. It is the love of Jesus Christ that laid Him in a tomb. His unequaled love paid the horrendous debt of sin for all mankind and claimed complete victory over the grave. It is because of His outstanding love (which conquers all) that we are able to be conquerors - and because of what Christ has done for us, we can boldly proclaim victory in every situation and over every sin.

2. **The Cross** – *By the cross we refer to the most common symbol of Christianity. It is intended to represent the death of Jesus when He was crucified on the True Cross and His resurrection in the New Testament (John 19:17 – 18).*

   At the time of Jesus' death, crucifixion was considered the most painful and degrading form of capital punishment in the Roman Empire. It was considered so horrible that it was used by the Romans exclusively for execution of slaves, those from the provinces under their control, and the lowest types of society's criminals.

   I now realize the more I appreciate and love that blessed cross, the more I appreciate and love God - which also grows my love for others. The same grace I so desperately needed and graciously received is the same grace others require in their lives. It was at the cross that I first saw the light; it was at the cross where the cumbersome burdens of my heart rolled away. It was there by faith, I received my sight. Oh, how I love that old rugged cross!

Although completely innocent of all sin, Jesus offered the most horrible and disgraceful punishment known. His agonizing death was no ordinary death, for it was not the final chapter. Jesus turned that apparent defeat into the most glorious victory the world has ever known. At the cross, He suffered for the sins of the entire world. Then, three days later after His resurrection from the dead, Jesus empowered His disciples with a new message - the Good News that He had finally defeated the power of sin and death. Through the cross, Jesus offers salvation to all who will believe in Him. Jesus' single sacrificial act richly poured God's love into our hearts (Romans 5:5-6).

3. **Relationship** - *When we refer to a relationship with the Lord, we refer to the very adoption of a sinner into the family of God whereby now they are called a son/daughter of the Most High (Ephesians 1:5). This adoption process takes place at the moment of salvation.*

If we don't know God (relationship), we cannot properly love Him or others (fellowship). Knowing God is not simply an intellectual proposition. You "know" God in a manner similar to the process of getting to know a human companion. Knowing God is a matter of personal involvement - mind, will, and feelings.

We (mankind) are dead in our sins without Jesus Christ. We are unable to express any form of godly love because God does not dwell within us. Before salvation, we do not have a relationship with our Creator; therefore, there can be no fellowship, intimacy, or love. Why not? Because God is love! I'm not referring to the 'world's' type of love, but rather the Great Shepherd gives a surrendering, valuable, and unreserved love. Everything He says and does...every thought and feeling stems from love. Without the indwelling of the Holy Spirit, we are not capable of properly loving God, others, or ourselves.

To "know" God refers to a deep experiential knowledge of God, rather than just information about Him. To get to know another person, you have to commit yourself to that person's company and interests - and be prepared to identify yourself with that person's concerns. Without it, your relationship can only be superficial and flavorless. It is impossible to know God intimately without loving others, for remember always: God is love!

Anyone in whom God dwells reflects His character. To claim to know God while failing to love others equates to making a false claim. Once we form a relationship with Jesus, we are never lonely. We never lack understanding or compassion. We can continually pour out our hearts to Him without being perceived as overly-emotional or pitiful. The Christian who truly shares a relationship with Jesus will never draw attention to himself, but will only show the evidence of a life where Jesus is in complete control.

4. **Fellowship** - *The close association experienced between Christ and the believer. This union places emphasis on the participation, sharing, contribution, gift, and outcome of such a close walk (1 John 1:3; 1 Corinthians 10:20).*

   The fourth key to truly loving God and our fellowman properly is found in an ever-increasing fellowship with God. As our fellowship with God deepens, we begin to see God, others, and ourselves in a different light. The closer we are to the Lord, we can begin to see things through His eyes - the way He sees things. That transforms the way we treat others, the way we think about others, and ultimately the love we have towards others.

   I can truly testify to that truth in my life. It was out of a deeper fellowship that I was led to write this material. It was out of a deeper fellowship that I am now able to see just how dark my heart was. It was out of a deeper fellowship that I can now see God for who He is - LOVE.

   Those who have yet to discover the fellowship of God often view Him as being cold and demanding toward His creation. Nothing is farther from the truth. Even in the Old Testament, we find God constantly moving towards mankind in an effort to reveal more of Himself on an intimate basis. Love motivates Him to do so.

In fact, love is the motivating factor of every true relationship.

- Love motivated the heart of God to not destroy man in the Garden of Eden.
- Love was the one thing that motivated Him to deliver Israel from the Egyptians.
- Love brought down the walls of Jericho.
- Love was the motivation behind the coming of Christ.
- Love took our place on Calvary's cross, and Love later rose from the grave.
- Love reaches out to us each day with freshness and hope.

You were created by love to live within its embrace. Many wonder how God could love them so deeply, but He does. He is Love, and He loves you and me.

5. **Intimacy** - *Intimacy is linked with feelings of closeness, safety, trust and transparency among partners in a relationship. For intimacy to be sustainable and nourishing it also requires trust, simplicity and acts of connection. Intimacy is both the ability and the choice to be close, loving, and vulnerable. Intimacy requires identity development. You must know yourself in order to share yourself with another.*

   What is God's greatest desire for you? God sees you as a precious treasure, and He longs to have a close relationship with you. More than anything, He wants you to have an intimate love relationship and friendship with Him. God wants you to spend time with Him and intimately communicate with Him, to enjoy fellowship with Him, to trust and follow Him, and to give your life meaning and purpose.

   The more time you spend with the Lord in fellowship and in meditation on His truth…the more time you spend in obedience to Him…the greater your passion to know Him…those things grow your intimacy. The Samaritan woman at the well discovered this principle in the short amount of time she spent talking to Jesus. When Jesus offered her living water, her curiosity was bothered. She was flooded with many emotions, including surprise and wonder. The woman was so excited about her new relationship, she left her water pot and ran to tell others in town (John 4:1-42).

That is what happens when you know the Lord: Your excitement grows and, with it, your fervor for sharing His Good News with others. As my intimacy with Jehovah deepens, so does my love for Him and others. The more time I spend with Him in fellowship, the more He reveals about Himself to me and the more He reveals about me. Seeing that God is love, the more I see of Him, the more love I see and experience. Seeing that His Spirit dwells within me, the more He reveals - and the more love I have to express. The more love I experience and express, the deeper my fellowship and intimacy grows. The deeper my fellowship grows, the more love I experience. It's what I like to call the "Perpetual Pursuit of Perfection". It's the great never-ending story!

All of the disciples followed and spent time with Jesus. All of them had a true, loving relationship and fellowship with Jesus (excluding Judas). However, Peter, James, and John shared an intimacy with Christ that the other nine did not obtain (Mark 9:2). I liken the experience this way: I know a lot of women. I have a relationship with certain women – but I have only one wife. I am only intimate with one woman: my wife. In the same way, I am exposed to an assortment of spiritual forces. I have connections with particular spiritual forces; but I only have one God. My soul is only intimate with the True and Living God.

"And when He came into the house, He suffered no man to go in, save Peter, and James, and John, and the father and the mother of the maiden" (Luke 8:51).

Closing Thought

"Good habits result from resisting temptation."
~ Unknown

My 6th Love Letter to God

(Use this section to be honest with both God and yourself. Tell God why you LOVE HIM, what you need forgiveness for, and why you are grateful.)

A FINAL WORD

"One minute of being honest with yourself is worth more than days, months, or years of self-destruction."
~ The 4th Secret of the One Minute Manager

NO
MAYBE
YES

The material you have just finished reading is not, by any means, a "cure-all". It will not solve all of your problems. It will not place you in perfect harmony with the Lord. First, this is an account of my personal journey towards loving God better. Secondly, this information will prayerfully lead you in the right direction; it will give you tools to work with and help you along life's journey.

At this moment, my life is not exactly what I desire – neither is it exactly what God desires. This one thing I do know: My life, my inner-man, and my intimacy with the Lord is so much better. Now that I realize where my sin originates, I know how to properly battle. As well, I now possess the weapons necessary to fight spiritual battles. Now that I recognize my true capacity to love God and others properly, my frustration towards myself is much less. Now that I can clearly see what real love is, I understand when I am operating from Jesus' love.

I challenge you, reader, to stop counting the number of times you have failed the Lord. That is a common distracting tactic of Satan to take our focus off the Lord. Look up into the eyes of God's eternal love where you can find unconditional acceptance (Ephesians 1:6).

Many often wonder: *How could a holy and just God accept such a wicked and perverse people?*

Many often wonder: *What does God want from us?*

Many often wonder: *What is God's will for our lives?*

Though we repeatedly make it complex, it is actually very simple: He desires for each of us to experience the goodness of His intimate love and personal care.

So, how do I answer the question that started all of this: *"Do you love Me or do you love the world?"* Yes, I do love the LORD! Although I don't always behave in a manner consistent with God's love, within my heart is a yearning to be free from the shackles of the sinful, unredeemed nature that is also within me. Deep within my heart is a longing to love the Lord my God with my entire mind, body, and soul.

Like many Christians, I have had to learn how to put first things first. One such Christian was Simon Peter (a disciple). In fact, Scripture reveals a lot about the inconsistencies of Peter's behavior and his many irrational decisions. The more time he spent with Jesus, the more he learned the difference between more activity and accomplishment. The more time he spent with Jesus, Peter learned the difference between man's ways and God's ways. Therefore, I must end in the place where I began: with Jesus Christ our Blessed Redeemer.

Most people don't want to reap the consequences of their actions. You can see that type of attitude everywhere. If we are to present ourselves before our Blessed Redeemer, we must be willing to accept the penalty of our actions. A Christian who is willing to take responsibility for their actions and be honest or "transparent" with God is someone the Holy Spirit can use. That Christian is also someone God can bless.

Ultimately, David became a great leader - not because he lacked limitations in life; he achieved much because he pushed past those limitations into the awesome presence of God. Therefore, like David, I must come back to our true source of life. Where else can I go? I shall always come back to Him crying, *"Father, save me!"* (Matthew 14:30); *"Jesus, forgive me!"* (Luke 15:21); and *"Holy Spirit, cleanse me of my sins!"* (Psalm 51:2).

The Apostle John noted those three powerful pulls (lust of the flesh, lust of the eyes, and the pride of life) that must be controlled. Those, he says, are not of the Father; they are of the world - therefore, they are not part of the standard we must strive to live according to. If we follow them, we will continue to be conformed to the world. God the Father would not say such a thing if it were not possible for us to be disloyal to God Himself, the Family of God, and the way of God.

Amazingly, within me still dwells an attraction for this world and for Satan. It is something I must constantly fight and put down. God instructed Israel often and in many ways against that type of productivity. Israel, though, was disastrously curious and incautious, filled with discontented, unsettled, impatient, and "grass is always greener" yearnings.

Just as He did thousands of years ago, Jesus calls us today to reject the natural human inclination towards self. The first step is to submit and surrender our will, our affections, our bodies, and our lives to God. Our own pleasures and happiness can no longer be primary goals. Instead, we must be willing to renounce all and lay down our lives - if required. Peter admonishes us to "no longer live…in the flesh for the lusts of men" - meaning we should no longer pursue wrong desires.

Are you willing to forsake all? Are you willing to give up everything including your life? Our Christian duty is to deny ourselves for the acceptance of Christ. Just as Adam was tested…just as Jesus was tried…just as Simon Peter was asked…God is still inquiring today: ***"Do you love Me?"***

Closing Thought

"The time is always right to do what is right."
~ Martin Luther King, Jr.

TEACHER'S OUTLINE

THE LUST OF THE FLESH (1 John 2:16)

1. The word "flesh" used in English describes our fallen nature and sinful tendencies. The Bible clearly tells us that our flesh is enemy with God.
2. We must not try to deal with sin habits in our own strength. Breaking sinful habits must be done in cooperation with the Holy Spirit and in dependence upon Him.
3. It is when we engage in physical activities outside of the will of God that they become sin.

A Lost Inheritance (Genesis 25:29-34)

1. We possess everything we will ever need in the Lord.
   a. We cannot allow our physical cravings to determine our actions.
2. Disobedience brings death to our lives and negates our spiritual birthrights.

The Fall of Solomon (1 Kings 11:1-6)

1. Solomon forgot the first principle of wisdom: "The fear of the Lord is the beginning of wisdom" (Psalm 111:10).
   a. When we link our lives with individuals who and possessions that are not God-centered, we send our lives into the hands of Satan.
   b. What have I joined myself to that is luring me away from God?
2. Taking many wives violated the standard of monogamy established by God.
   a. Each Christian should have one God, and God should have one cohesive unit of believers.

   b. Jesus clearly instructs us: We cannot have two masters.
   c. We must allow Jesus Christ to be Lord over every area of our lives!
3. The type of love Solomon possessed for his wives refers to romantic love and covenant loyalty.
   a. Because his wives did not follow God and Solomon was "tied" to them, his heart was led astray.
   b. God continually warns us to not associate with a particular people because they do not have a relationship with Him.
4. Solomon compromised his faith by worshipping foreign gods.
   a. Our association with the world always harms us in the end.
5. God instructs us that we should have no other god before Him.
   a. We must follow the Lord with our entire being.
   b. This does not mean you will not make mistakes. It does mean we won't cover up our mistakes, make excuses, or be unwilling to repent.
   c. A heart that is quick to repent is a true sign of a maturing believer.

In the Beginning – Good for Food (Genesis 3:6)

1. Eve was drawn or tempted by the idea of the fruit being good for food.
2. Although she could see nothing wrong with the fruit, a great danger was present.

Jesus' Temptation - Israel's Wilderness (Luke 4:3-4; Deuteronomy 8:3)

1. Knowing that Jesus had gone weeks without food, Satan used Jesus' natural desire for food to suggest He should use His supernatural powers to create food and eat it.
    a. Lust of the flesh can be very difficult to combat because it fights against our very nature of self-preservation.
2. Jesus knew that food was necessary for a person's physical needs. He also knew that obedience to the Father was far more important.
    a. Our powers are limited; therefore, our abilities to satisfy are limited as well.
    b. Our powers and abilities are temporary; therefore, our capacity to satisfy is temporary.
3. Life in the wilderness had taught Israel that our existence depends on more than the food people eat.
    a. Our existence depends upon spiritual forces that are found only in God.
4. Countless men and women strive to fulfill their physical cravings by their own methods.
    a. All our needs - even physical needs - can be met only in the presence of the Lord.

Everyday Jesus (John 4:31-35)

1. Physical food is very necessary to sustain our physical being, but it is not the only thing we need.
    a. We live by every Word that comes from the mouth of God (Matthew 4:4).
    b. For Jesus, it was necessary (meat) to do the will of God.

Our Solution (Galatians 5:16-17, 24-25)

1. "Walk" actually means to live in the Spirit.
    a. We are to conduct our lives as people being influenced by God's Holy Spirit.
    b. The only consistent way to overcome our sinful desires is to live step-by-step in the power of the Holy Spirit.
2. Christians are spiritually "crucified".
    a. They no longer have to follow the values or desires of the world.
    b. Jesus tells us that if we love Him, we will possess a heart of obedience.
3. That type of walk is to follow, to adhere, and to listen to the encouragements of the Holy Spirit.
    a. "Walk in the Spirit" means to obey the promptings of the Holy Spirit.

THE LUST OF THE EYES (1 John 2:16)

1. Our eyes, thoughts, and imaginations make up the lust of the eyes.
2. That can also include what we hear, think, and/or meditate upon in our minds.

David's Wandering Eyes (2 Samuel 11:2-4)

1. David committed a series of sins that brought him much sorrow and trouble.
    a. We must be mindful that our actions hold great consequences throughout all eternity.
    b. David was guilty of sexual immorality with Bathsheba - wife of Uriah, one of David's top soldiers.
    c. He tried to cover his mistakes by means of murder (none of his schemes worked).

2. David's problems started when his "eyes" left the Lord and began to become fixed on Bathsheba.
    a. The lust of the eyes draws us away from the Word of God and devours our confidence in God.

Herod's Lustful Eyes (Matthew 14:3-10)

1. Our eyes and ears greatly determine our thought life.
    a. Television, radio, and even our thoughts can be sources of distraction.
2. We cannot allow Satan to "hypnotize" us with the lure of temptation.

In the Beginning – Pleasant to the Eyes (Genesis 3:6)

1. The lust of the eyes was instrumental in the fall of man.
    a. The fruit on the Tree of Knowledge was pleasant to the eyes.
    b. It was of a beautiful color and very inviting.
2. If man could take his "eyes" off of his desire, he could resist temptation.
    a. The longer we look at our lustful desires, the greater the desire becomes for it and, at the same time, the weaker our will becomes to obey our Creator.

Jesus' Temptation – Israel's Wilderness (Luke 4:5,8; Deuteronomy 6:13)

1. Satan's temptation towards Jesus was clearly an empty attempt to stir the visual senses of the Almighty.
    a. The showing tempted the natural eyes of Jesus as the luscious fruit tempted Eve in the Garden of Eden.

2. We often follow the very thing that is forbidden.
    a. Of all the hundreds of trees in the garden that could've been eaten, mankind desired the one thing that was off-limits.
3. Above all things, God desires to have a loving relationship with us.
    a. God feels pain and grief when we forget Him or when we turn away from Him to follow idol gods.
    b. We find full satisfaction through walking humbly before God and keeping His law.
4. The nation of Israel grieved God's heart by chasing after gods and withholding their devotion and adoration from Him.

Everyday Jesus (Luke 7:12-13; Matthew 18:9)

1. Jesus was not moved by egotistical greed, lust, power, or pride.
    a. Far too often, we look at individuals with the wrong motives and intentions.
2. He looked on her with compassion.
3. Jesus is not teaching us to dismember our physical bodies. He is instructing us to place nothing before Him.
4. Anything that causes us to sin against God must be done away with.
    a. We are to be on a constant spiritual guard.

Our Solution (Job 31:1; Matthew 5:28; Proverbs 6:25-29)

1. A person who gazes upon another with the purpose of wanting them sexually has mentally (and in their heart) committed adultery.
    a. Like murder, adultery is the final fruit of wrong thoughts and uncontrolled feelings.

2. The eye, as well as the rest of the body, must be brought under control – whatever the cost.
    a. Temptation must be cut off at the source; the inward man.
    b. If our eyes are looking, our minds are thinking.
3. We do not face temptation alone.
    a. Jesus provides the strength you need to say "no" to every dark thought or evil imagination.
4. Being tempted is not a sin.
    a. Even Jesus was tempted (Luke 4:1-13).
    b. Sin is the result of acting on the temptation.
    c. God always provides the strength we need to steer clear of temptation.

THE PRIDE OF LIFE (1 John 2:16)

1. The pride of life consists of arrogance and boasting of self.

King Saul's Mess (1 Samuel 15:12-19)

1. Pride can very easily creep into our lives undetected.
    a. The higher the Lord elevates us, the greater the responsibility (Luke 12:48).
2. Willful disobedience can be another form of pride.

King Uzziah's Destruction (2 Chronicles 26:15-16)

1. As long as Uzziah followed God, the Lord helped Him.
    a. Sadly, that God-given success made Uzziah proud.
2. If you are looking down on people, you cannot be looking up to God.
    a. Pride always leads to regretful shame.

Fighting Against God (James 4:6)

1. God fights against those who operate from a prideful outlook.
    a. The home, our work, and the church all suffer because of pride.
2. When you function out of pride, you have elected the alternative by default.

In the Beginning – Desirable to Make One Wise (Genesis 3:6; Isaiah 14:12-14)

1. Pride was the most engaging motive to influence Eve to eat of the tree.
    a. It was an eager desire for more wisdom and knowledge.
2. The Apostle Paul counted everything he knew as nothing compared to the knowledge of Christ.
    a. We must not allow anything to separate us from the love of Christ.
3. The virtue opposite of pride is humility.
    a. It is through pride that Lucifer became Satan.
    b. Pride leads to every other vice.
    c. Pride is a complete anti-God state of mind.
    d. Satan's fall was caused by the indulgence known as pride.

Jesus' Temptation – Israel's Wilderness (Luke 4:9, 12; Deuteronomy 6:16)

1. Jesus could have been very frustrated at the world's refusal to accept Him.
2. Satan believed he had an opportunity to bring Christ down with that information.

3. To tempt (test) is to try one with a good or evil intent.
    a. Satan and evil people test others when they put their virtue to the test with the aim of seducing them into sin.
    b. People are said to test God when they put His patience, faithfulness, or power to the test.
    c. Our Father encourages us to come to Him with our humble requests, but not to complain.
4. The Israelites contended with their God-given leader, Moses.
    a. Contend is used by the prophets to describe a judicial dispute.
    b. It means a grumpy complaining, very similar to the Israelites' murmuring.

Everyday Jesus (Philippians 2:5-7)

1. If you are going to live right, your mind must be renewed.
    a. Right thinking produces right actions.
    b. Our actions are the fruit of our deepest thoughts, whether good or bad.
2. The term "slave" is the lowest status on the social ladder and is the exact opposite of the term "lord".
    a. The Lord chose to be a servant.
    b. While remaining completely God, He became completely human.
3. Jesus is our perfect example of how to live as a servant.
    a. God is in search of hearts that are completely surrendered to Him.
    b. He is seeking those who are available, dependable, and willing to be used.
    c. God will not force you to serve Him. You must be a willing servant.

Our Solution (2 Chronicles 33:11-13; 1 Peter 5:5-7)

1. When we fight against God, we fight a losing battle.
    a. God often allows captivity to humble us.
2. Humility is defined as to be subdued or to bring down.
    a. God views pride as an abomination (Proverbs 16:5).
        i. Abomination is a word that refers to God's disgust.
3. God cherishes and honors a humble, repentant spirit.

THE LOVE OF JESUS (1 Corinthians 13; John 15:9-10, 12-14, 17)

1. 1 Corinthians 13 is one of the Bible's most extensive explanations of what God's love is.
2. If people are true disciples of Christ, they will prove it by their love.
    a. We must possess and demonstrate the love of Jesus.

Jesus' Love Towards Us (Romans 5:8)

1. While we were still enemies of God, He loved us.
    a. God loves us just the way we are, but He loves us too much to leave us the way we are.
2. Regardless of life's circumstances, God loves you.

We Must Follow His Example (Ephesians 5:1)

1. Believers are to follow the example of God's actions.

Our Love Towards Others (John 13:34-35)

1. Moses said, "Love your neighbor as yourself" (Leviticus 19:18).
2. Jesus said, "…as I have loved you".
    a. The same way Jesus has loved you, you are to love others.
3. Whatever we do to others is what we offer to God (Matthew 25:40).
    a. The world will identify you as a Christian by your love.

Giving is Essential in True Love (John 3:16; 1 John 3:18)

1. We cannot profess to be loving children of God if we are not a giving people.
    a. Our Father is not stingy, nor are His people stingy.
    b. Love is an action that is to be lived.
2. Believers need to share with those in need (Matthew 25:34-40).
    a. When we express God's love, we will be people of action.

Finally, Love One Another (1 Corinthians 13:4-8)

1. The Word of God clearly tells us what God's love is and is not:
    a. **Longsuffering (patient):** The love of Jesus patiently bears frustrations and is not quick to stress its rights and is not quick to be offended by an injury (Matthew 27:39-43).
    b. **Love is kind:** Those who express the love of Jesus will convey pleasant deeds to help – not deeds of hurt (Acts 10:38).

c. **Love does not envy:** A negative attitude of lust and desire for another's possessions (Mark 9:38-40).
d. **Not puffed up:** Is not proud (that is the root of boasting). Love is modest and humble (John 5:19).
e. **Love does not behave rudely:** To act improperly, dishonorably, indecently, or rudely (Matthew 5:17).
f. **Not her own will:** Is not self-seeking (Matthew 26:39).
g. **Rejoices in the truth:** Corresponding to reality (John 17:17).
h. **Bears all things:** To put up with, stand, to protect, cover (John 1:29).
i. **Believes all things:** Love expects the best from people (John 5:14).
j. **Hopes all things:** An attitude of confidently looking forward to what is good and beneficial (Luke 22:31-32).
k. **Love never fails:** Love wins in every situation. No matter the circumstances, love is the answer (John 3:16).

DO YOU LOVE ME? (John 21:12-19)

1. Agape love is a selfless love; the type of love which characterizes God.

a. Agape is a love that only the Lord of Hosts is able to show. John affirms that by saying, "God is love" (1 John 4:8).
b. God does not merely love; He is love. He loves us simply because He has chosen to do so.

2. Phileo love is affection and regard of a very high order.
    a. Phileo love is a strong fondness, to treat affectionately or kindly, to strongly like.
    b. The love Simon spoke of was nothing more than the fondness found in a casual friendship.

In the Beginning – A Test of Love (Genesis 3:1-6)

1. Satan has always tested our love for the Father.
    a. Jesus said: "If you love me, you'll keep my commandments" (John 14:15); "Why call me your Lord and do not as I say?" (Luke 6:46); "If you do as I say, you'll abide in my love; just as I've kept my Father's commandments, and abide in His love" (John 15:10).
2. There will always be temptation vying for our hearts, but we must decide who or what we love the most.
    a. When it comes to God and the things of this world, there is only one correct choice.
    b. Love is never complex when it comes to God.
    c. He only desires that we love Him with our whole mind, whole body, and whole soul.

Jesus' Temptation – A Test of Love (Luke 4:1-13)

1. Everyone faces temptation.
2. Every problem and concern that we may have is a struggle with a decision.
    a. God has presented us with life and death through our choices.
3. Satan is limited by the power God allows him to possess.
    a. Sin is a choice. Satan can tempt us, but we decide to sin.
    b. The battle is already won against Satan.

Jesus' Victory (Luke 22:42)

1. We must be careful to make choices that coincide with the will of God.
2. Feelings and emotions are usually not the best guides for making decisions.

Everyday Jesus (John 15:9-10)

1. We must give up all to accomplish the will of God.
2. God's love is not based on the merit of the recipient (Romans 5:7-8).
3. The Lord is concerned with every large and small aspect of our lives.

Our Solution (1 John 4:7-8, 15-16)

1. There are five key areas that will assist us in our journey to properly loving God:
    a. **Salvation** – (Romans 10:1-4)
    The first step in knowing the Lord is found in what Christ has done for us. If we cannot accept what His Son has done for us, we cannot and will not love the Lord and others.

    This is what must be done for you to be saved from your sin:

        i. Admit you are a sinner in need of a Savior (Romans 3:23).
        ii. Believe what Jesus has done for you (Romans 5:8).
        iii. Confess with your mouth what you believe (Romans 10:13).

b. **The Cross** – (John 19:17-18)
    i. As our love and appreciation for the cross grows, so does our love for God and others grow.
    ii. Jesus suffered the most horrible punishment known.
        1. Jesus turned defeat into the most glorious victory the world has even known.
        2. Through the cross, Jesus offers salvation to all who will believe in Him.
        3. With His single act, God's love is richly poured into our hearts (Romans 5:5-6).

c. **Relationship** – (Ephesians 1:5)
    i. If we don't know God (relationship), we cannot properly love Him or others (fellowship).
        1. You "know" God in a manner much similar to the process of getting to know a human companion.
        2. Without the indwelling of the Holy Spirit, we are not capable of properly loving God, others, or ourselves.
    ii. To know God refers to a deep experiential knowledge of God, rather than just information about God.
        1. To get to know another person, you have to commit yourself to his company and interests – and be ready to identify yourself with his concerns.

d. **Fellowship** – (1 John 1:3; 1 Corinthians 10:20)
   i. We must strive to possess an ever-increasing fellowship with God.
      1. As our fellowship with God deepens, we begin to see things in a different light.
   ii. True fellowship with God will help you see that He is a loving and personal God (not cold and distant).
      1. Love motivates the Lord in all He does.

e. **Intimacy** – (Luke 8:51)
   i. More than anything, the Father wants you to have a close, loving relationship and friendship with Him.
      1. God wants you to spend time with Him and intimately communicate with Him.
   ii. The more time you spend with the Lord in fellowship, meditation, and obedience to Him, the greater your passion to know Him.
      1. That builds intimacy.
   iii. The more intimate time you spend with Him, the more He reveals to you about Himself and the more He reveals about you.

BIBLIOGRAPHY

Blanchard, K. and Johnson, S. (2008). *The 4th Secret of the One Minute Manager: A Powerful Way to Make Things Better.* Harper Collins Publishers (U.S.).

Made in the USA
Middletown, DE
12 April 2016